Ausgabe des Sanskrittextes und seiner tibetischen Übertragung im Vergleich mit den chinesischen Übersetzungen. Von Hiromi Habata. Marburg 2007. lxxv, 203 S.

52. *Pāsādikadānaṁ.* Festschrift für Bhikkhu Pāsādika. Hrsg. von Martin Straube, Roland Steiner, Jayandra Soni, Michael Hahn und Mitsuyo Demoto. Marburg 2009. xxvii, 511 S.

53. *Untersuchungen zum Udānavarga.* Unter Berücksichtigung mittelindischer Parallelen und eines tibetischen Kommentars. Von Michael Balk. Marburg 2011. 516 S. [Nachdruck der Dissertation von 1988]

54. *Le théâtre de l'Inde médiévale entre tradition et innovation : Le Moharājaparājaya de Yaśaḥpāla.* Par Basile Leclère. Marburg 2013. 614 pp.

55. *Subhūticandra's Kavikāmadhenu on Amarakośa 1.1.1–1.4.8.* Together with Si tu Paṇ chen's Tibetan translation. Edited and introduced by Lata Mahesh Deokar. Marburg 2014. xv, 588 pp.

56. *Subhūticandra's Kavikāmadhenu on Amarakośa 1.4.8cd–2.2.5ab.* Together with Si tu Paṇ chen's Tibetan translation. Edited and introduced by Lata Mahesh Deokar. Marburg 2018. xiii, 740 pp.

57. *Compounds and Compounding in Old Tibetan.* A Corpus Based Approach. By Joanna Bialek. Marburg 2018. 2 vols. 586 + 610 pp.

58. *Bhāskarakaṇṭhas Cittānubodhaśāstra.* Kritische Edition der ersten drei Kapitel nebst Erstedition des Autokommentars. Von Stanislav Jager. Marburg 2018. xv, 407 S.

59. *Unearthing Himalayan Treasures.* Festschrift for Franz-Karl Ehrhard. Edited by Volker Caumanns, Marta Sernesi, and Nikolai Solmsdorf. Marburg 2019. xxiv, 488 pp.

60. *Sāhib Kaula's Tree of Languages.* A multilingual carmen cancellatum from 17th century Kashmir. By Jürgen Hanneder. Marburg 2021. x, 124 pp.

Weitere Publikationen des Verlages

- *Āyurveda und Poesie.* Lolimbarājas Lehrgedicht »Leben des Arztes« (*Vaidyajīvana*). Herausgegeben und übersetzt von Jürgen Hanneder und Thomas Schäfer. Marburg 2018. 113 pp.
- *Sanskrit-Vademecum.* Von Maximilian Mehner und Jürgen Hanneder. Marburg 2019. 92 pp.
- *Walter Slaje: Kleine Schriften zur kaschmirischen Kultur- und Geistesgeschichte.* Hrsg. von Jürgen Hanneder, Andreas Pohlus und Roland Steiner. Marburg 2019. 2 Bände. xxxii, 883 S.

* * *

Indica et Tibetica Verlag
Lindenstr. 24, D-35287 Amöneburg, Germany
post@iet-verlag.de | http://www.iet-verlag.de

36. *Bauddhasāhityastabakāvalī.* Essays and Studies on Buddhist Sanskrit Literature Dedicated to Claus Vogel by Colleagues, Students, and Friends. Edited by Dragomir Dimitrov, Michael Hahn, and Roland Steiner. Marburg 2008. xxvi, 351 pp.

37. *Vividharatnakaraṇḍaka.* Festgabe für Adelheid Mette. Herausgegeben von Christine Chojnacki, Jens-Uwe Hartmann und Volker M. Tschannerl. Swisttal-Odendorf 2000. 540 S.

38. *Das Kompendium der moralischen Vollkommenheiten.* Vairocanarakṣitas tibetische Übertragung von Āryaśūras *Pāramitāsamāsa* samt Neuausgabe des Sanskrittextes. Von Naoki Saito. Marburg 2005. x, 412 S.

39. *Aspekte des Weiblichen in der indischen Kultur.* Herausgegeben von Ulrike Roesler. Swisttal-Odendorf 2000. xii, 192 S.

40. *Mārgavibhāga* – Die Unterscheidung der Stilarten. Kritische Ausgabe des ersten Kapitels von Daṇḍins Poetik *Kāvyādarśa* und der tibetischen Übertragung *Sñan ṅag me loṅ* nebst einer deutschen Übersetzung des Sanskrittextes. Von Dragomir Dimitrov. Marburg 2002. xiii, 395 S.

41. *Das Pāṇḍulohitakavastu.* Über die verschiedenen Verfahrensweisen der Bestrafung in der buddhistischen Gemeinde. Neuausgabe der Sanskrit-Handschrift aus Gilgit, tibetischer Text und deutsche Übersetzung. Von Nobuyuki Yamagiwa. Marburg 2001. 255 S.

42. *Prinz Goldglanz auf der Reise durch Himmel und Höllen.* Zwei japanische Bildrollen des *Bishamon no honji* aus dem 16. Jh. im Kölner Museum für Ostasiatische Kunst. Beschrieben und ausgedeutet von Katja Triplett. Marburg 2001. 130 S.

43/1. *Āryaśūras Jātakamālā.* Philologische Untersuchungen zu den Legenden 1 bis 15. Teil 1. Einleitung, Textausgabe, Anhänge, Register. Von Albrecht Hanisch. Marburg 2005. lxxxvii, 255 S.

43/2. *Āryaśūras Jātakamālā.* Philologische Untersuchungen zu den Legenden 1 bis 15. Teil 2. Philologischer Kommentar. Von Albrecht Hanisch. Marburg 2005. ix, 409 S.

44. *Aspects of the Female in Indian Culture.* Proceedings of the Symposium in Marburg, Germany, July 7–8, 2000. Edited by Ulrike Roesler and Jayandra Soni. Marburg 2004. ix, 182 pp.

45. *Texte zum Vājapeya-Ritual. Maitrāyaṇīsaṃhitā* 1.11 und *Taittirīyabrāhmaṇa* 1.3.2–9 mit Bemerkungen zu *Kāṭhakasaṃhitā* 13.14 und 14.1–10. Eingeleitet, übersetzt und kommentiert von Karin Steiner. Marburg 2004. 125 S.

46. *Prinz Sudhana und die Kinnarī.* Eine buddhistische Liebesgeschichte von Kṣemendra. Texte, Übersetzung, Studie. Von Martin Straube. Marburg 2006. xiv, 269 S.

47. *Jaina-Itihāsa-Ratna.* Festschrift für Gustav Roth zum 90. Geburtstag. Herausgegeben von Ute Hüsken, Petra Kieffer-Pülz und Anne Peters. Marburg 2006. ix, 522 S.

48. *Nāgārjuna's Ratnāvalī, Vol. 3. Die chinesische Übersetzung des Paramārtha.* Herausgegeben, übersetzt und erläutert von Yukihiro Okada. Marburg 2006. x, 260 S.

49. *Lehrschrift über die zwanzig Präverbien im Sanskrit.* Kritische Ausgabe der *Viṃśatyupasargavṛtti* und der tibetischen Übersetzung *Ñe bar bsgyur ba ñi śu pa'i 'grel pa* (Editionen von Texten der Cāndra-Schule. Band I). Von Dragomir Dimitrov. Nach Vorarbeiten von Thomas Oberlies. Marburg 2007. vii, 123 S.

50. *Kuvalayamālā.* Roman jaina de 779 composé par Uddyotanasūri. Vol. I : Étude; Vol. II : Traduction et annotations. Par Christine Chojnacki. Marburg 2008. 393 + 784 pp.

51. *Die zentralasiatischen Sanskrit-Fragmente des Mahāparinirvāṇa-Mahāsūtra.* Kritische

213 S.

18. *Hundert Strophen von der Lebensklugheit.* Nāgārjunas Prajñāśataka, tibetisch und deutsch. Eingeleitet, herausgegeben und übersetzt von Michael Hahn. Bonn 1990. 124 S.

19. *Nāgārjuna's Ratnāvalī. Vol. 2. Die Ratnāvalīṭīkā des Ajitamitra.* Hrsg. und erläutert von Yukihiro Okada. Bonn 1990. xxxv, 198 S.

20. *Ḍākinīs.* Zur Stellung und Symbolik des Weiblichen im tantrischen Buddhismus. Von Adelheid Herrmann-Pfandt. 2., erweiterte Auflage. Marburg 2001. xv, 600 S., 11 Abbildungen.

21. *Frank-Richard Hamm Memorial Volume.* October 8, 1990. Ed. by Helmut Eimer. Bonn 1990. 215 pp.

22. *Studien zur Indologie und Buddhismuskunde.* Festgabe des Seminars für Indologie und Buddhismuskunde für Professor Dr. Heinz Bechert zum 60. Geburtstag am 26. Juni 1992. Herausgegeben von Reinhold Grünendahl, Jens-Uwe Hartmann und Petra Kieffer-Pülz. Bonn 1993. 326 S.

23. *Der Lobpreis der Vorzüglichkeit des Buddha.* Udbhaṭasiddhasvāmins Viśeṣastava mit Prajñāvarmans Kommentar. Nach dem tibetischen Tanjur herausgegeben und übersetzt von Johannes Schneider. Bonn 1993. 333 S.

24. *Dvāviṃśatyavadānakathā.* Ein mittelalterlicher buddhistischer Text zur Spendenfrömmigkeit. Nach zweiundzwanzig nepalesischen Handschriften kritisch herausgegeben von Mamiko Okada. Bonn 1993. xxii, 239 S.

25. *Tibetan Studies.* Jan Willem de Jong. Swisttal-Odendorf 1994. ix, 254 pp.

26. *Unterscheidung der Gegebenheiten von ihrem wahren Wesen (Dharmadharmatāvibhāga).* Eine Lehrschrift der Yogācāra-Schule in tibetischer Überlieferung. Von Klaus-Dieter Mathes. Swisttal-Odendorf 1996. iv, 296 S., 11 Falttafeln.

27. *Sukṛtidatta Pantas Kārtavīryodaya.* Ein neuzeitliches Sanskrit-Mahākāvya aus Nepal. Von Johannes Schneider. Swisttal-Odendorf 1996. 430 S.

28. *Suhṛllekhāḥ.* Festgabe für Helmut Eimer. Herausgegeben von Michael Hahn, Jens-Uwe Hartmann und Roland Steiner. Swisttal-Odendorf 1996. xxiii, 283 S.

29. *Die Gilgitfragmente des Kāraṇḍavyūha.* Herausgegeben von Adelheid Mette. Swisttal-Odendorf 1997. 164 S.

30. *Bauddhavidyāsudhākaraḥ.* Studies in Honour of Heinz Bechert on the Occasion of His 65th Birthday. Edited by Petra Kieffer-Pülz and Jens-Uwe Hartmann. Swisttal-Odendorf 1997. 759 pp.

31. *Untersuchungen zu Harṣadevas Nāgānanda und zum indischen Schauspiel.* Von Roland Steiner. Swisttal-Odendorf 1997. 319 S.

32. *Licht und Leuchten im Ṛgveda.* Untersuchungen zum Wortfeld des Leuchtens und zur Bedeutung des Lichts. Von Ulrike Roesler. Swisttal-Odendorf 1997. xi, 286 S.

33. –

34. *Studia Tibetica et Mongolica.* (Festschrift Manfred Taube). Redigenda curaverunt Helmut Eimer, Michael Hahn, Maria Schetelich et Peter Wyzlic. Swisttal-Odendorf 1999. xxix, 342 S.

35. *Sūryacandrāya.* Essays in Honour of Akira Yuyama on the Occasion of His 65th Birthday. Edited by Paul Harrison and Gregory Schopen. Swisttal-Odendorf 1998. xiv, 265 pp.

INDICA ET TIBETICA (IeT)

Monographien zu den Sprachen und Literaturen des indo-tibetischen Kulturraumes

1. *Nāgārjuna's Ratnāvalī. Vol. 1. The Basic Texts (Sanskrit, Tibetan, Chinese).* By Michael Hahn. Bonn 1982. vi, (34), 208 pp.

2. *Das Maitrakanyakāvadāna (Divyāvadāna 38).* Sanskrittext und deutsche Übersetzung. Von Konrad Klaus. Bonn 1983. 108 S.

3. *Das Mṛgajātaka (Haribhaṭṭajātakamālā XI).* Studie, Texte, Glossar. Von Michael Hahn und Konrad Klaus. Bonn 1983. iii, 108 S.

4. *Five Buddhist Legends in the Campū Style.* From a collection named *Avadānasārasamuccaya.* Edited and translated (with an introduction) by Ratna Handurukande. Bonn 1984. (63), 234 pp.

5. –

6. *Nächtliches Wachen.* Eine Form indischen Gottesdienstes. Von Monika Thiel-Horstmann. Bonn 1985. 126 S., 3 Tabellen.

7. *Die Śīghrabodhinīnāmamālā des Puṇḍarīka Viṭṭhala.* Ein synonymisches Wörterbuch des Sanskrit aus dem 16. Jahrhundert. Herausgegeben und übersetzt von Ardo Schmitt-Rousselle. Bonn 1985. 160 S.

8. *Ārya-Śūra's Compendium of the Perfections.* Text, translation and analysis of the Pāramitāsamāsa. By Carol Meadows. Bonn 1986. x, 371 pp.

9. *Die altindische Kosmologie.* Nach den Brāhmaṇas dargestellt. Von Konrad Klaus. 2., unveränderte Auflage. Marburg 2004. 197 S.

10. *Lehrbuch der klassischen tibetischen Schriftsprache.* Siebte, korrigierte Auflage. Von Michael Hahn. Marburg 1996. xiv, 376 S.

10a. *Schlüssel zum Lehrbuch der klassischen tibetischen Schriftsprache* und *Beiträge zur tibetischen Wortkunde (Miscellanea etymologica tibetica I–VI).* Von Michael Hahn. Marburg 2003. 150 S.

11. *Vicitrakusumāñjali.* Volume Presented to Richard Othon Meisezahl on the Occasion of his Eightieth Birthday. Ed. by Helmut Eimer. Bonn 1986. xiv, 146 pp.

12. *Towards a New Edition of Ārya-Śūra's Jātakamālā.* By Peter Khoroche. Bonn 1987. 76 pp.

13. *Indology and Indo-Tibetology.* Thirty Years of Indian and Indo-Tibetan Studies in Bonn. Ed. by Helmut Eimer. Bonn 1988. 192 pp.

14. *Emendationen zum Jaiminīya-Brāhmaṇa (Zweites Buch).* Von Gerhard Ehlers. Bonn 1988. xxxv, 135 S.

15. *The Supriyasārthavāhajātaka.* Edited with an introduction by Ratna Handurukande. Bonn 1988. 105 pp.

16. *Das Kaṭhināvadāna.* Eingeleitet, herausgegeben und übersetzt von Almuth Degener. Bonn 1990. vi, 103 S.

17. *Der Tantra-Katalog des Bu ston im Vergleich mit der Abteilung Tantra des tibetischen Kanjur.* Studie, Textausgabe, Konkordanzen und Indices. Von Helmut Eimer. Bonn 1989.

साहिबकौलविरचितः कल्पवृक्षः

Sāhib Kaula's Tree of Languages

A multilingual carmen cancellatum from 17th century Kashmir

By

Jürgen Hanneder

Indica et Tibetica Verlag
Marburg 2021

Bibliographische Information der Deutschen Nationalbibliothek
Die Deutsche Nationalbibliothek verzeichnet diese Publikation in der Deutschen Nationalbibliografie; detaillierte bibliografische Daten sind im Internet über http://dnb.dnb.de abrufbar.

Satz: Jürgen Hanneder
Herstellung: BoD – Books on Demand, Norderstedt, Germany

ISSN 0723-3337
ISBN 978-3-923776-66-5 (Hardcover)
ISBN 978-3-923776-67-2 (eBook)

सा	हि	त्या	म्बु	नि	धौ	गा	ढे	सा	हि	
ब्कौ	ल	प्र	मा	थि	नि	अ	पू	र्व	म	
कृ	त	ज्यो	त्थं	वा	णि	वै	चि	त्र्य		
क	ल्प	कं	ले	ख	नं	त	स्य			
वृ	क्ष	स्य	प	टे	रे	ख	वि	चि	त्रि	ते
मु	द्र	णं	प्र	थ	मं	पू	र्णं			
त	स्ये	ह	सं	वि	धी	य	ते			

sāhityāmbunidhau gāḍhe sāhibkaulapramāthini
apūrvam akṛta jyottham vāṇivaicitryakalpakam
lekhanaṃ tasya vṛkṣasya paṭe rekhavicitrite
mudraṇaṃ prathamaṃ pūrṇaṃ tasyeha saṃvidhīyate

(Note: *jyottha* = *kṣitija*)

When the vast ocean of literature was churned by Sāhib Kaula,
he created a novel tree with the concept of many languages.
The writing of this tree onto a cloth full of lines
is printed here completely for the first time.

Preface

AT THE WORLD SANSKRIT CONFERENCE held 2012 in New Delhi the *Indira Gandhi National Centre for the Arts* presented a small exhibition. One item was the reproduction of a large cloth,[1] onto which a grid was painted that resembled an oversized chess-board. Each square contained one, sometimes more syllables in small Śāradā script so that the whole—to be read roughly 150 squares from left to right and 150 lines down—constituted one large continuous text. Some syllables were written in red ink and form patterns, so that diagonal, zigzag, square, rhombic and other red shapes were covering the whole cloth. These red texts, the so-called intexts,[2] could be read in various ways by following the red paths in different directions, and turned out to be mostly in Sanskrit, but some others seemed to be in Indian vernaculars, others could not be read at all.

My colleague Advaitavadini Kaul, since she knew that I was editing works of the Kashmirian author Sāhib Kaula, asked me whether I could make sense of the object, which was supposed to be a text by the same author, but I could not. In the following years, whenever I got access to manuscripts of the *Kalpavṛkṣa*, which was the name associated with this cloth, I had another look, but since these manuscripts were puzzling in many ways, the idea of editing the text was postponed more and more. There were too many questions surrounding this enigmatic object.

In the meantime Alessandro Battistini, who had worked on *citrakāvya*, had found out that three of these cloths existed, and very kindly forwarded scans and his photographs to me. So I pursued the matter further, found and collated more

[1] One accession card of the *National Mission for Manuscripts*, New Delhi, gives 155cm width. [2] The term is adopted from the elaborate vocabulary for visual poetry used in Ernst, *Carmen figuratum: Geschichte des Figurengedichts von den antiken Ursprüngen bis zum Ausgang des Mittelalters*. For details see below, p. 54.

sources, but too many unsolved questions surrounded the cloth so that I did not dare to publish any of the meagre results. It was only at the end of 2018 that I perused a manuscript—a huge codex of more than a thousand folios with materials on the Kaulas—which on a few pages turned out to contain the missing link. Suddenly Sāhib Kaula's "wish-fulfilling tree" started to make more sense. The new findings are spectacular enough to be relevant not only to a larger community of Indologists, but also to interdisciplinary research on *carmina figurata*, for, as will become clear in the following, the *Kalpavṛkṣa* seems to be the largest *carmen cancellatum* in world literature. It also most likely holds at least one other record, namely the one for the number of languages for the intexts. Nevertheless the text is keeping, as it were, quite a few secrets that are clearly beyond my expertise, to itself, and thus I consider my foundational work done and leave the remaining riddles to others.

Over the years many colleagues contributed in one or the other way to this work. I am very grateful to Advaitavadini Kaul for asking the question that I am now trying to answer, and of course for the set of scans, for Alessandro Battistini for providing further scans and pictures, to Oliver Kahl for identifying the Arabic text, and to Anna Martin for identifying the Persian text. Monika Horstmann, Hans Harder and Lata Deokar kindly shared their obervations on the non-Sanskritic texts with me. Dragomir Dimitrov very kindly put the partial scans together to form the complete picture, so that I could regularly stand in front of and ponder the object in a reproduction in original size. Thanks are also due to Stanislav Jager and Roland Steiner for proof-reading and to the editors of the *Mokṣopāya*, Susanne Stinner and Anett Krause, for access to the collation of the unpublished section of the *Nirvāṇaprakaraṇa*. Martin Gansten has kindly helped in the discussion and calculation of Indian dates, and with Hamsa Stainton, who has been working on Sāhib Kaul and his pupils, I had the pleasure of discussing some finer details around the literary history of the Kauls. And finally, the *Staatsbibliothek zu Berlin – Preußischer Kulturbesitz, Orientabteilung* and the *Niedersächsische Staats- und Universitätsbibliothek Göttingen* have kindly given their permission to reproduce the relevant manuscripts.

The work is dedicated to the memory of my *kāvyaguru* Michael Hahn, who would have been thrilled by the *Kalpavṛkṣa*.

Jürgen Hanneder

Contents

Preface vii

Contents ix

Overview 1

The Base Text 5
The Sources . . . 6
Text and Auto-commentary . . . 12
Two Versions of the Introduction in the Commentary . . . 12
The Introduction to the Commentary . . . 16
The Metrical Part . . . 18

The Intexts 23
The Sources . . . 24
The Old Cloth (C_1) . . . 24
The 19th century Śāradā Cloth (C_2) . . . 25
The Nāgarī Cloth (C_3) . . . 25
Some Examples for Intexts . . . 27
Other Intexts in Sanskrit . . . 37
The Colophon of the *Kalpavṛkṣa* . . . 38

The Wish-fullfilling Tree of Languages 41
The Language of the Author . . . 43
Classifying the *Kalpavṛkṣa* . . . 44
The *Kalpavṛkṣa* as *citrakāvya* . . . 45

The *Kalpavṛkṣa* as a *carmen cancellatum* 54
Conclusion: The Hidden Context 59

Manuscript Hs. or. 12509 63
"Indische Sammelhandschrift" – A brief overview 63
Facsimile Edition 76

The Beginning of the *Kalpavṛkṣa* with Auto-commentary 89

Bibliography 115
Manuscripts of the *Kalpavṛkṣa* 115
Printed Sanskrit Editions 116
Secondary Literature 119

Index 123

Overview

There are quite a few works of the seventeenth-century Śaiva author Sāhib Kaula available in manuscript libraries,[1] but whereas his *Devīnāmavilāsa* has been published long ago in a reliable edition,[2] the rest of his œuvre has remained mostly unknown.[3] With the recent availability of larger numbers of Kashmirian manuscripts[4] a much clearer picture of the author and his works started to emerge.

Sāhib Kaula[5] was active during the second half of the seventeenth century and was a prolific writer, according to Sanderson "the Kauls' most outstanding and influential author".[6] While his sometimes elaborate colophons provide some information about his family and his teachers, his works show that he subscribed to a mixture of Advaita Vedānta and Kashmirian non-dual Śaivism.

The author has mentioned a number of his works in the colophons of his *Devīnāmavilāsa*, not all of which are available in manuscript. At present we know of twenty works from the pen of Sāhib Kaula. Three are ritual handbooks written, compiled or merely associated with the author.[7] The above-mentioned *Devīnāmavilāsa* is a large *stutikāvya*, the *Citsphārasārādvaya* is a soteriological dialogue between teacher and student,[8] many other works are Stotras or something in between Stotras and religious poems. Among these the *Saccidānandakandalī* stands

[1] For details on sources and more background information see my forthcoming edition: Hanneder, *Sahib Kaula's Works.* [2] *The Devīnāmavilāsa. By Sāhib Kaul.* Ed. by Madhusūdan Kaul Shāstrī Lahore 1942 (Kashmir Series of Texts and Studies LXIII). [3] The print of some of his smaller works by Janardan Pandey in a collection of Śaiva works (Pāṇḍeya, *Śaivādvayaviṃśatikā*) cannot be counted, for it is so faulty as to give an unfavourable impression of the author. [4] For instance the eGangotri collection on archive.org. [5] The "Sāhib", by the way, is invariable part of his name and is spelt, reflecting the Kashmirian variation in spelling foreign words, as Sāhib, Sāhiba, even Sāhibha. Within his Stotras he calls himself *sāhibkaula.* [6] Sanderson, "Kashmir," p. 124. [7] *Śrīvidyānityapūjāpaddhati, Śyāmāpaddhati* and *Hṛllekhāpaddhati.* See Hanneder, *To edit or not to edit*, p. 221ff., for a discussion of this type of authorship. [8] See Hanneder, *To edit or not to edit*, p. 215–220.

out as being transmitted in Sanskrit and in a Bhāṣā version. Then we have the *Śivaśaktivilāsa*, *Sahajārcanāṣaṣṭikā*, *Nijātmabodha*, *Śivajīvadaśaka* and the *Śārikāstava*, which contains a *mantroddhāra* of the Kaula's lineage goddess (*vaṃśadevatā*).[1]

But the most unusual and enigmatic of Sāhib Kaula's works is clearly the *Kalpavṛkṣa*, written according to the colophon on the 12th August, 1676. The text is transmitted in a few manuscripts, to be briefly described below, but there are also three versions of the text written onto a large cloth. There the text of the *Kalpavṛkṣa*—identical with the text we know from the "normal" manuscripts—is filled into a grid from left to right and top to bottom. Some letters are written in red ink to form a net of red lines in all directions, containing apparently further layers of text, which we call intexts. The cloths are of considerable size[2] with a numbered chess-board grid of ca. 150 × 150 painted onto them. Lines and rows are numbered, and minute digits are running from the left top to the right and downwards.

The *mūla*-text of the *Kalpavṛkṣa* as known from the manuscripts,[3] the "linear" or "base" text—in contradistinction to the intexts, the paratexts in red ink—is filled into this grid. As far as the base text is concerned, the cloth is just like a giant one-page manuscript.

Strangely the editor of the *Devīnāmavilāsa*, who prides himself with being from the family of the author, and who has mentioned the *Kalpavṛkṣa* in his short description of Sāhib Kaula, has not given any hint about the content or nature of this work. Perhaps he had only seen the manuscripts of the text, but not the cloths. Admittedly there is not much in the manuscripts to alert the reader to the fact that this is but the base text of a piece of visual art, which can only be properly understood and appreciated when viewing the cloth.

[1] See Hanneder, "Śārikā's Mantra." [2] One accession card of the *National Mission for Manuscripts*, New Delhi, gives 155cm width. [3] The sources are given in some detail below, and part of the edition is reproduced at the end of this work.

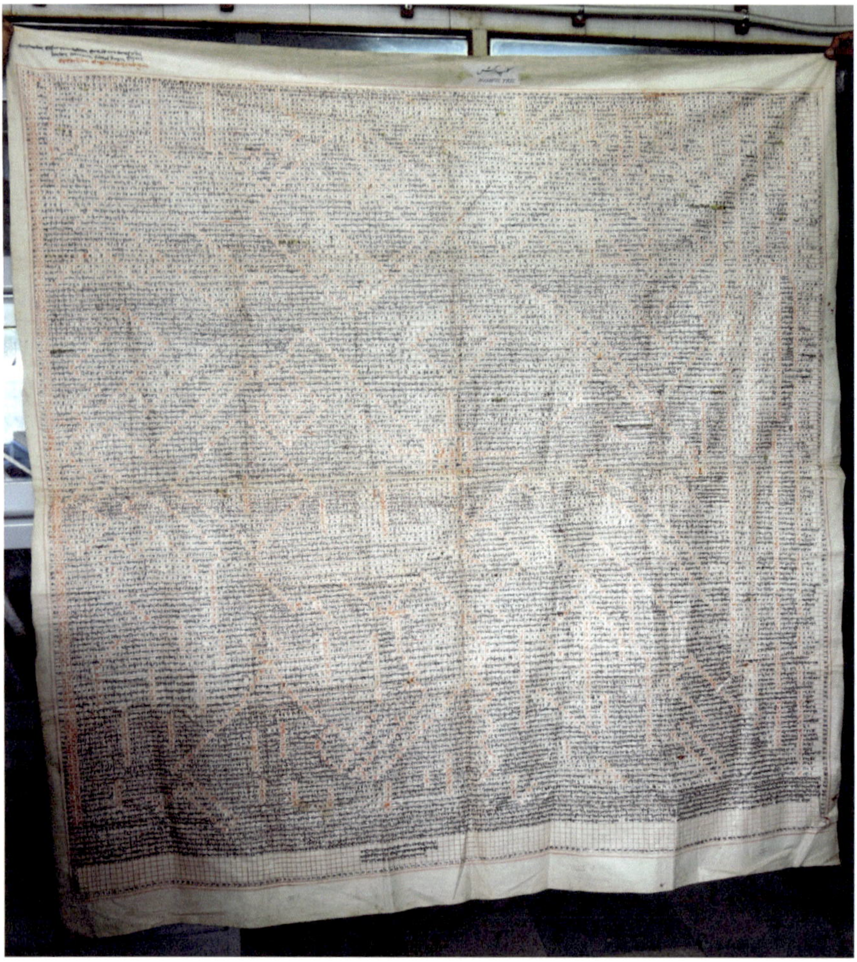

The *Kalpavṛkṣa* (Śāradā script on cloth)

The most spectacular feature of this visual poetry is not its enormous size, but the fact that the red intexts were written with the unstated but obvious aim to present as many languages as possible. Among them are familiar and unfamiliar names from the subcontinent, even Persian and Arabic. Since the Sankritic sphere was

usually quite reluctant to allow anything foreign into their literary orb, this is all the more noteworthy, and it is not astonishing to find this in Kashmir.[1]

The *Kalpavṛkṣa* as a specimen of figurative poetry has two types of Indian antecedents or contexts. As far as the use of multiple languages is concerned, we have the so-called *bhāṣāśleṣa*s, of which there are earlier examples. However, these are limited to a verse being formulated in a way that it can be read in Sanskrit as well as in one or more literary Prakrits or (Kashmirian) Apabhraṃśa.[2]

The other context is the classical Indian genre that encompasses figurative poetry, that is, *citrakāvya*. Apart from subsuming various types of verbal artistry in general, in one of its types, poetry is written into certain shapes, which usually involves a complicated way of non-linear reading.[3] Examples are highly artistic, but like Kāvya itself are concentrated on the single stanza as the unit. But there are fundamental differences: the *bhāṣāśleṣa* format is limited to syllables or words identical in both languages. Here the cross-word mechanism is more flexible and can accommodate other languages, as long as a transcription method is used that does not exceed the pool of syllables that can be used in Sanskrit.

Finally, the fact that the literary representation of thirty languages was accomplished in the remote and sometimes secluded valley of Kashmir may come as a surprise, but while Kashmirian borders might have been at times physically insurmountable, the intellectual exchange with the outside world was obviously quite vivid.

[1] For instance, all three instances of translations or adaptations of literary works from Persian to Sanskrit are from Kashmir. See Hanneder, *To edit or not to edit*, p. 34ff. [2] See Hahn, "Der Bhāṣāśleṣa. Ein Besonderheit kaschmirischer Dichter und Poetiker?" For a Jaina example, see Vose, "Jain Uses of Citrakāvya and Multiple-Language Hymns in Late Medieval India: Situating the Laghukāvya Hymns of Jinaprabhasūri in the 'Assembly of Poets'," pp. 312ff. [3] For a more detailed analysis see below, p. 45.

The Base Text

The text of the *Kalpavṛkṣa* is composed in a sometimes complicated and enigmatic style that is quite typical of the author. As his œuvre shows, Sāhib Kaula is able to write perfectly understandable verses, but his predilection for alliterations can occasionally cloud the sense. I give one instance from the metrical part of the *Kalpavṛkṣa*:

> *aśeṣaṃ nirviśeṣaṃ ca viśeṣaṃ śeṣaśeṣitam*
> *nirastasakalakleśaṃ mahaḥ svaṃ sad upāsmahe* (165)

While the main sentence in the second line "We adore our own being, the light that has brushed aside all defilements" is fairly clear, the many conceivable ways to interpret the adjectives in the first line may somewhat confuse a translator. Of course one can find "literal" or other plausible translations, and apart from the unusual *śeṣaśeṣitam* the commonplace words should not be a problem. But once one has read more of the author, and knows that he cannot bypass a chance for a double entendre, we start to think about whether *vi-śeṣa* should not be interpreted etymologically as *vi(gata)śeṣa* and so forth. Knowing more of the author has severely complicated the process of interpretation.

We find similar word plays throughout his works, and it was to be expected that the *Kalpavṛkṣa* would contain similar passages, but here—to make things worse—in a long-winded prose style, as the very first sentence of the text shows:

> *śrīmacchrīsvasvatantrānāśritanirbhāgaparamaprakāśavimarśamaya-*
> *pāramaiśvaryānubhāvānubhāvukaprathitamahitanijasahajaparamā-*
> *nandādvayasattāsāmānyaspanda uditoditaparamaśaktisāmrājyo*
> *rājarājeśvaro jayasi paramaśivas tvam ayam.*

Again a basic and more literal translation may not be too difficult, since the main clause is transparent: "You, this Paramaśiva, are victorious". The rest are attributes further qualifying the subject Śiva. And exactly there the problematic details of interpretation start to surface. Is *rājarājeśvara* a mere name? Surely not, especially not in a Śāstra where every word is overloaded with doctrinal details. And similarly the two pronouns *tvam ayam* are in need of a doctrinal interpretation, for the literal one does not make much sense. The first two longer compounds are perhaps easier, for they can be interpreted in a Śaiva framework, and the long compound is most likely a string of standard adjectives qualifying Śiva. He is independent (*svatantra*), unapproached (*anāśrita*), consisting of supreme light and reflection (*paramaprakāśavimarśamaya*) and so on. All these terms have more or less standardised exegetical interpretations, but are taken in his auto-commentary as the starting point for a commentator's tour de force. But before dealing in more detail with text and auto-commentary, we shall briefly introduce the sources.

The Sources

The *Kalpavṛkṣa* is one of the larger works of Sāhib Kaula and can be read as a philosophical treatise without even knowing that it forms the base text of a kind of crossword. It has a manuscript transmission that is separate from the cloth versions in the sense that unless one knows that this is a text originally written into a large grid, nothing in the text will alert one to this fact.

This *mūla*-text consists of a lengthy prose part, followed by 230 verses and a conclusion and colophon again in prose. There is an auto-commentary that consists of an introduction and three sections of commentary, each on just one sentence of the *mūla*-text's prose beginning, in other words on merely a tiny fraction of the complete text. To complicate matters, there is a longer and a shorter version of the beginning of the commentary.

There are five manuscripts, only two of which (B_3, $Ś_2$) contain the complete *mūla*-text. Some manuscripts, which only transmit the beginning of the text ($Ś_2$, G_2, $Ś_1$, B_4), have in addition an auto-commentary just on the beginning of the text. If more was ever written of the commentary, it is not transmitted.

These are the manuscripts:[1]

$Ś_1$ Jammu, Dogra Art Museum 425		birch bark, Śāradā
$Ś_2$ Śrīnagar, Oriental Research Library 1353		Paper, Śāradā
G_2 Göttingen, Cod. Ms. Sansc. Vish 203		Paper, Śāradā
B_3 Berlin, Hs. or. 12460		Paper, Śāradā
B_4 Berlin, Hs. or. 12666		Paper, in Nāgarī and Śāradā

The commentary extends only to the first three prose passages, which together correspond to one folio side out of 90, counting from the Berlin manuscript (B_3) that transmits the complete *mūla*-text. The present edition of this part—one folio of mūla plus commentary— amounts to no less than 18 pages. It is unclear whether Sāhib Kaula has commented only on the beginning, or whether the remainder is lost, in which case the work would have been his most voluminous one.

For the bulk of the *mūla*-text, we have one very interesting manuscript B_3 (Berlin Hs. or. 12460). It is written with exceptional clarity, it even adds clarifications in case of unusual word divisions, makes use of the *avagraha*, in some parts even regularly, and there are at first sight no discernible errors. Furthermore the manuscript is in a perfectly legible hand so that one would wish that all Śāradā manuscripts were like it. There are some corrections by another hand, so the manuscript makes the impression of being proofread. But as usual, as soon as we collate it with a second source and ponder over variants, it turns out to be just as fallible as any other source.

Coming to the commentary manuscripts, we might expect most from manuscript $Ś_1$, which is written in Śāradā on birch bark, for in general the use of birch bark predated the use of paper in Kashmir. The birch bark manuscript is closely related to B_4, which contains exactly the same text, and is partly written in Nāgarī (first eight folios), partly in Śāradā on paper. It transmits many of the misreadings of the birch bark version, but sometimes also adds minor corrections to the text. In the Nāgarī section its variants are often mere errors in transcription.[2] Such errors are plenty and they are trivial in the sense that they result in meaningless readings that can be explained by the paleographical peculiarities of the Śāradā style of $Ś_1$. For instance, we find the word *gadyapadyatrayeṇa* in B_4

[1] "Göttingen" refers to Niedersächsische Staats- und Universitätsbibliothek, Göttingen, "Berlin" to Staatsbibliothek zu Berlin, Preußischer Kulturbesitz. [2] For instance, *saṃskṛtapada* becomes *saṃskṛtamada*.

as a misreading for *gadyapadyakrameṇa* in Ś$_1$. The scribes obviously had no eye for what they were copying, in one passage, a scribe writes *granthakṛt svamadyaṃ vivṛṇoti,* but the author here does not explain his drink, what he means of course is "his verse" (*svapadyaṃ*).

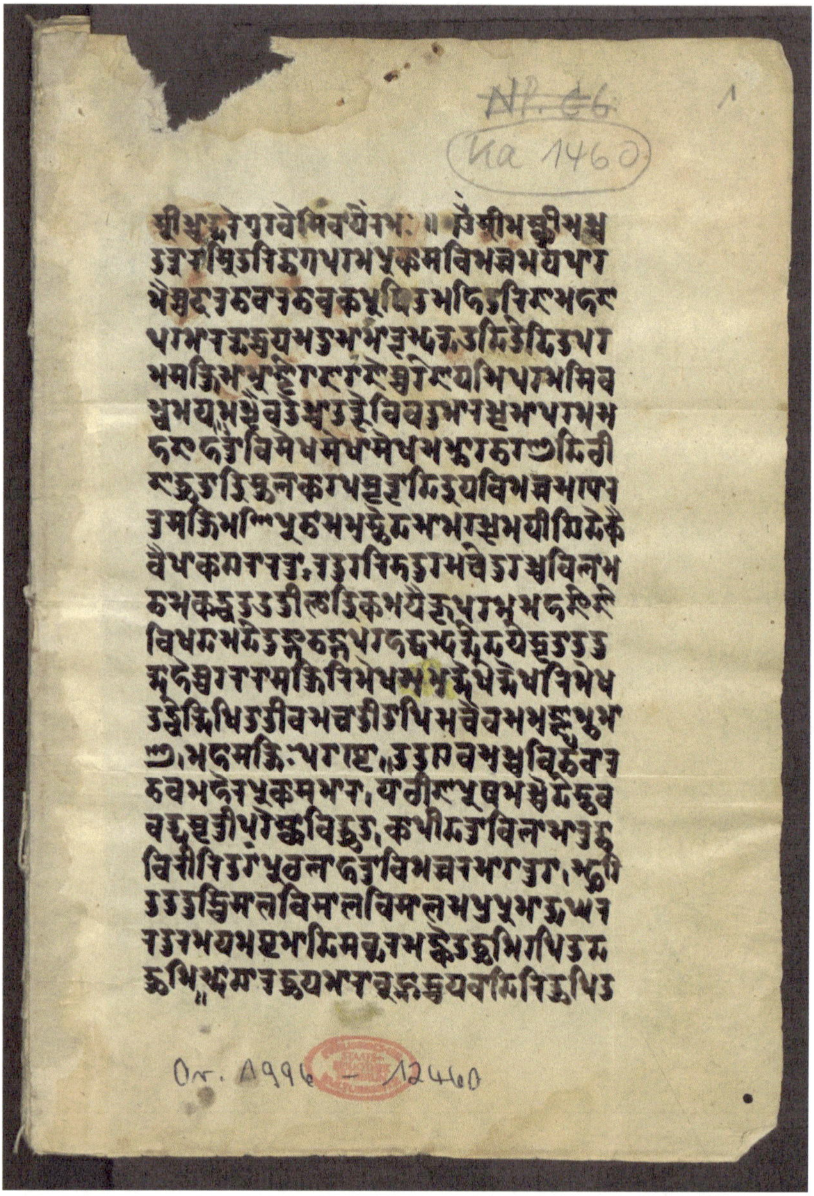

Beginning of B_3, folio 1^r

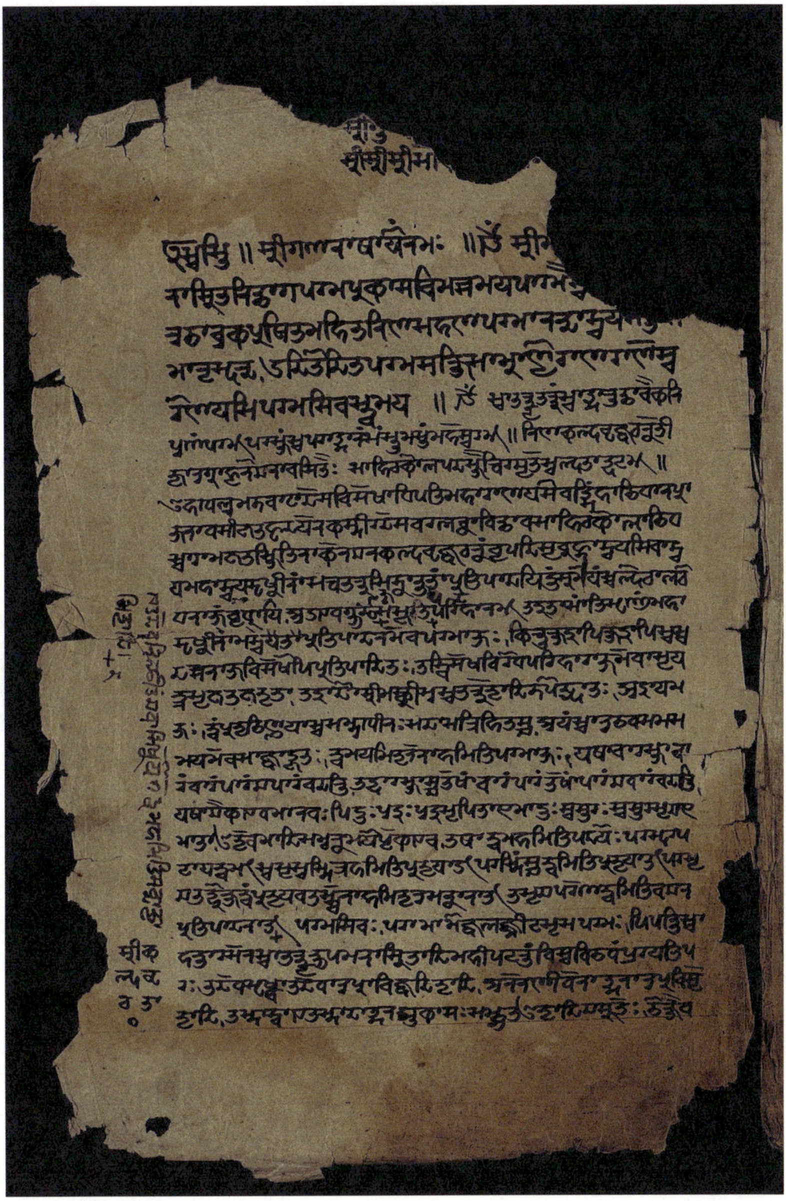

Beginning of G₂ 1[r]

Unfortunately $Ś_1$ is very erroneous in many places. It omits *visargas*, produces haplographies (*upātteḥ* for *upapatteḥ*) and other errors that suggest a combination of ignorance of the text with carelessness by the scribe. Then there are cases, where B_4 supplies what is missing, or corrects minor and obvious slips of the pen in his archetype: B_4 reads the correct *granthādau* for the *ganthādau* of $Ś_1$. The older birch bark manuscript thus unfortunately does not contain the superior text one might expect.

From a comparison of the mss. we ought to deduce that $Ś_1$ and B_4 go back to the same archetype. Both are extremely close, but have their own peculiar misreadings. Furthermore the way the words are divided within compounds and other idiosyncrasies shared by the two manuscripts are best explained by a close common ancestor. But there is one constellation that enables us to actually identify the ancestor. In two places B_4 and $Ś_1$ indicate a gap that is identical with a marginal break-off in G_2, so it is highly probable that the ancestor was no other than G_2. Furthermore, G_2 has usually a convincing text and would have to be followed, whatever the genealogical relation. What is unexpected is that here a birch bark manuscript ($Ś_1$) is an apograph of a surviving paper manuscript (G_2)! The constellation does not amount to an actual and usable stemma, but is quite limited, since the manuscripts preserve different versions of the introduction and thus display contamination on a larger scale.

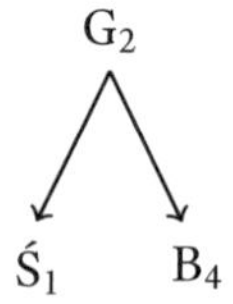

We should also mention that the text of $Ś_2$ has been transcribed and made available online in the Muktabodha Digital Library. For the present edition this was not of much help, since the transcript contains too many substantial misreadings to be of use. This is due to the difficult hand of this manuscript and most probably a certain unfamiliarity with the Śāradā alphabet, which resulted in confusing misreadings: *śavramṛṣṭi*, for instance, was in fact clearly legible in the manuscript as *śabdasṛṣṭi.*[1]

[1] In practice the errors add up to produce a hardly understandable text. Compare the Muktabodha version of the first verse in the introduction: *nijakalpavṛkṣavandetīkyāna grāhyanodanāvaśitaiḥ / sāhibakaulapadasthairviraśyate svalpatāt padam? //*

Text and Auto-commentary

The edition of the *Kalpavṛkṣa*, the beginning of which is appended to this volume, produces a hybrid text, for it combines the complete *mūla*-text with (two versions) of the commentary. There is no manuscript with this constellation. The only practical problem resulting from this is that it is unclear where the *mūla*-text originally stood in the commentary manuscript, and whether our hybrid text should start with the first sentence of the *mūla*-text, or with the introductory verse of the commentary. The edition follows the Göttingen manuscript by starting with the first prose sentence of the *mūla*-text. Then follow the two versions of the introduction by the author to his auto-commentary, then the first section with commentary, the second section with commentary and the third section with commentary. Thereupon follows the large remainder of the no less difficult *mūla*-text—but without a commentary.

Two Versions of the Introduction in the Commentary

The briefer version of the commentary contains two introductory verses followed by a prose passage that specifies the cause for writing the *mūla*-text as well as the author's aim in writing the commentary.

> *svātantryatantraṃ svātmāntarbhāvaikanipuṇaṃ param*
> *parasthaṃ svaparātmānaṃ saṃstumas taṃ maheśvaram*
> *nijakalpavṛkṣabandhe tīrthyānugrāhyanodanāvaśitaiḥ*
> *sāhibakaulapadasthair viracyate svalpatātparyam*

iha khalu maruvāṭadeśaviśeṣādhipatimahārājayaśovatsiṃhābhidhānaprārthanāvaśīkṛtahṛdayena kaśmīradeśavaralabdhāvirbhāvasāhibakaulābhidhasvārāmakṛtasthitinā kenacana kalpavṛkṣabandhaṃ vyapadiśya brahmādvayaśivādvayamahādvayadṛṣṭīnāṃ sarvatantrasiddhāntatāṃ pratipādayituṃ śramo 'yaṃ svalpo bālabodhanārthaṃ vyadhāyi/

> We adore the supreme Maheśvara, who is dependent on independence, clever at living inside one's self, who resides in the supreme reality (*parastha*), who is the self of me and everyone else.

> Residing in the state of (being) Sāhib Kaula, I shall compose a brief commentary on my composition *Kalpavṛkṣa*, having been impressed by requests that should be favoured (*anugrāhya*) also by *tīrthyas*.[1]
>
> The person, who resides (*kṛtasthiti*) in his "*ārāma*" called Sāhib Kaula, which appeared in the great land of Kashmir, who having been entreated[2] by the ruler of the land of Marvar (*maruvāṭa*), called Mahārāja Yaśovat Siṃha, devised[3] the composition *Kalpavṛkṣa*, here (i.e. with this commentary) makes some effort to explain for the sake of enlightening the uneducated (*bāla*) that Advaita Vedānta, Śaiva non-dualism and supreme non-dualism all are the final conclusion of all philosophical systems.

The introductory verse states in no unclear terms that Sāhib Kaula has written a commentary on his own work, which conveniently puts at rest the question of authorship. It also shows the philosophical aim—or is this hinting more at the politics of religion?—of claiming a close connection or allegiance of the three types of non-dualism. What is less clear is the author's reference to himself. For introducing his name and person Sāhib Kaula uses a variety of formats in his works, ranging from first person (*so 'haṃ saṃvyadadhaṃ*), to third person (*sāhibakaulaḥ cakāra*), and to passive constructions. Less obvious are phrases stating that the author "resides in the" *pada*, *āśrama* or *ārāma* called Sāhib Kaula.[4] While the first word seems to point to a religious interpretation, the two last terms seem to point to a more realistic interpretation of a "garden" (*ārāma*) or "hermitage" (*āśrama*), named after the author as "Sāhib Kaula". The word *sāhibakaulapada* would then be in fact a *śleṣa* meaning "the state of being Sāhib Kaula", but also "the place called Sāhib Kaula", which refers to the "Sāhib Kaula Garden".

---

[1] It is not clear what the author means by *tīrthya*. Assuming the usual sense of "heretic", we would have to pinpoint the group to which it refers. Walter Slaje has suggested to me that it refers to Muslims, since Kashmir was at the time part of the Moghul empire. There is another passage – to which Hamsa Stainton has alerted me – namely Govinda Kaula's *Gurustutiratnāvalī*, vs. 3, where the beneficiaries are mentioned, onto which Sāhib Kaula is "showering his nectar rain", most probably referring to his teaching: *suramunipitṛkān kārmikāṃs tīrthyasaṅghān*. This might point into the same direction, to literally "groups of heretics, who hold offices", which might mean Muslims in Kashmirian administration.

[2] Simplified translation for *-prārthanāvaśīkṛtahṛdayena* "whose heart has been captivated by the entreaty of [...]". [3] The word could imply the "trick" involved in the work. [4] *so 'haṃ sāhibkaulakārāmaśambhuḥ Śivajīvadaśaka* 1, *sāhibkaulārāmasusthena Śivajīvadaśaka* 11, *sāhibkaulapadasthena Saccidānandakandalī* 101, *māheśvarācāryavareṇa sāhibkauläspadasthena Svātmabodha* 51.

While the shorter introduction consists just of two introductory verses and one sentence, the longer version takes up four pages. It starts with a longer version of the same sentence, then follows another introductory verse (*sveṣṭeśī-*) which is then explained in great detail. After this the author promises to return to the topic at which point the two verses from the shorter introduction are quoted, as if part of the main text. The detailed relationship between the two versions thus remains difficult, except that in all likelihood one is the revised version of the other. That it was written by anyone but the author himself is I think unlikely.

This is the beginning of the longer version:

iha khalu maruvāṭadeśaviśeṣādhipatiśrīmanmahārājayaśovatsiṃhābhidhānaprārthanāvaśīkṛtahṛdayena śrīmatkaśmīradeśavaralabdhāvirbhāvaśrīmacchrīsamagrakaulaśiromaṇisvacchatarasamastaṣaḍdarśanasiddhāntasārāgraṇyamahāntaḥkaraṇena śrīmatsāhibakaulābhidhasvārāmakṛtasthitinā kenacana kenāpi cidvilāsena brahmādvayaśivādvayamahādvayadṛṣṭīnām advaitatāpratipādanapuraḥsarāṃ sarvatantrasiddhāntatāṃ pratipādayitum asya śrīkalpavṛkṣābhidhaprabandhasya gadyapadyādivākyaracanāracitasya śākhāphalapuṣpādiracanāracitasyeva sākṣātkalpataroḥ prāk prarohaṃ samullikhitavatā tathā cāhamādhvanikas tatkulajātimān bālānām iva svalpabuddhināṃ tadvicāraniḥśreṇisamārohaṇāśaktānāṃ gūḍhārthasaṃskṛtapadaparisphoṭanāya tattadviśeṣavirodhaparihānāya ca nijakāruṇyadṛṣṭyā tatsvalpatātparyaracanāvidhau kaṭākṣitaḥ san yathāmati vyākaromīti tatra tāvadgranthādau vighnadhvaṃsanapūrvakasamāptikāmaḥ sveṣṭadevatānamaskāralakṣaṇaṃ maṅgalaṃ vidadhyān manasi vihitam api saddṛṣṭyapāṭhakānuśāsanāya gadyapadyakrameṇa chandasopanibadhnīyāc ceti śiṣṭir ācāraś cety etanmatam āśritya granthakṛt svapadyaṃ vivṛṇoti sveṣṭeśīti //

In the beginning only two honorifics are added, but then there are numerous additions: Sāhib Kaula is called "crown jewel of all Kauls" and so forth. Unfortunately the construction of the whole passage does not add up. It starts with a passive construction as in the shorter version, but after *samullikhitavatā* the *anvaya* is lost: there is an active construction (*ahaṃ […] yathāmati vyākaromi*), which is merely a quotation, but the whole passage ends with *granthakṛt svapadyaṃ vivṛṇoti sveṣṭeśīti*. In other words, the construction remains an anacoluthon. It is tempting to regard this longer introduction as written by a redactor, but the different positioning of the verses does not allow us to further redact the whole passage

into a meaningful whole. There is also no indication that the commentary that follows could be by anyone but the author, so I rather assume a failed redaction.

The reason why the longer introduction is crucial for the interpretation of the whole work, is the following passage:

> [...] *śrīkalpavṛkṣābhidhaprabandhasya gadyapadyādivākyaracanāracitasya śākhāphalapuṣpādiracanāracitasyeva sākṣātkalpataroḥ prāk prarohaṃ samullikhitavatā* [...]
>
> [...] painting first the aerial roots[1] of this composition called *Kalpavṛkṣa*, which is written in a composition of sentences in prose and verse,[2] as if[3] of a real (*sākṣāt*) wish-fullfilling tree consisting of a composition of branches, fruits, blossoms, etc., [...]

I had regularly discussed the images seen on the cloth with colleagues, and once or twice the idea of aerial roots was mentioned, which I considered and discarded. The reason was my deficient understanding of the above passage, but since *praroha* is actually attested as aerial roots, this gives not only a clue to the translation of the above passage, but also to the whole *figura* of our *carmen figuratum*. Even if the physical resemblance is not as striking as one might expect, the red lines can be interpreted to represent the aerial roots of a *Kalpavṛkṣa*, in analogy with one of the most magnificent trees of the subcontinent, the Banyan (*vaṭa*, *ficus benghalensis*).

The other unexpected information given in the introduction is of course that on the plausible recipient of the cloth—if this is the implication of Sāhib Kaula "being entreated" by the king to compose the work.

Sāhib Kaula dedicated the *Kalpavṛkṣa* to *Yaśovat Siṃha* (Jaswant Singh), ruler of *maruvāṭa*, modern Marvar, who reigned from 1638 to 1678. It is likely that this piece of visual art was composed for and presumably presented to the ruler of Marvar.[4] This is an unexpected glimpse into a historical context not known from anywhere else. I am not aware of any other reference in the works of Sāhib Kaula to this ruler. Connections of this area to Kashmir are known from an earlier source: Śrīvara in his *Rājataraṅgiṇī*[5] mentions Rāja Mānsingh of Amber (1540–1614). The

---

[1] I take *praroha* in the sense attested (only) in SCHMIDT's *Nachträge*: "Luftwurzel". [2] The *ādi* can hardly have a literal sense here. [3] I provisionally regard the *iva* as *bhinnakrama*. [4] By the way the historical reference contained in the work is lost in the Muktabodha transcript, where we read *mahārājayamevat siṃhābhidhāna*, whereas in the manuscript we actually find *mahārājayaśovatsiṃhābhidhāna*. [5] Additional verse ad 1.7.174

circumstances under which Sāhib Kaula was entreated by the ruler to write this composition are unknown. We know, however, that Jaswant Singh can be ranked as a "vernacular intellectual"[1] who wrote on Advaita Vedānta in Brajbhāṣā. Like Sāhib Kaula he composed a number of religious works in dialogue form, and seems to demonstrate by the scope of his works a fusion of the literary and the religious spheres. Perhaps Sāhib Kaula wanted to connect to this movement of vernacular poetry supported at the Rajput courts of Rajasthan and it is perhaps for this reason that his *Saccidānandakandalī* is transmitted with a *bhāṣā*-version.

The Introduction to the Commentary

The longer introduction makes it clear that the introductory verse starting with *sveṣṭeśī-* is explained by the author himself, thereby again confirming authorship. The commentary is elaborate and gives all sorts of options of construction: The first word *sva-iṣṭa-īśī* is the goddess desired by "myself" (*svasya iṣṭā*) or by everyone in a group (*sveṣām iṣṭā*). Besides giving detailed commentaries on each word, the author explains the purpose of the work in the first four pages of the introduction.

Most importantly the introduction tells us something about the intended content of the work. The passage is hidden in the lengthy digression occasioned by the commentary on the *maṅgala* verse in the longer version of the introduction. At the end of this the author says: "Now enough of this prolixity concerning the *maṅgala* verse. We shall now pursue the topic." (*alaṃ tāvan maṅgalācaraṇe bahuvistareṇa, idānīṃ prakṛtam evānusarāmaḥ*). Only a little later this topic is, after an earlier brief reference, detailed again: "In this work the supreme truth (or ultimate aim) is mainly the demonstration of non-duality of the three above-mentioned three great philosophical views." (*tatra tāvat pūrvoktānāṃ tisṝṇām eva mahādṛṣṭīnām advaitapratipādanam eva paramārthaḥ*). These were indeed mentioned in the first introduction as *brahmādvaya*, *śivādvaya* and *mahādvaya*, which means the Vedāntic and Śaiva types of non-dualism, with an added "great" or "supreme" non-dualism that encompasses even dualism(s).

Then follows the commentary on the first prose passage, the so-called *preface* (*upodghāta*), which has been quoted in the beginning of the commentary, and is now merely referred to as a pratīka. This is the complete passage:

[1] See Williams, "Sacred sounds and sacred books: A history of writing in Hindi."

> *śrīmacchrīsvasvatantrānāśritanirbhāgaparamaprakāśavimarśamayapāramaiśvaryānubhāvānubhāvukaprathitamahitanijasahajaparamānandādvayasattāsāmānyaspanda uditoditaparamaśaktisāmrājyo rājarājeśvaro jayasi paramaśivas tvam ayam.*

The commentary decodes the text in much detail and with many options, starting with the last two words:

> "[The word] 'you' means the one who is present to the self through recognition and is always near. This ('you') is realized at the time of a personal[1] experience." (***tvaṃ*** *pratyabhijñayā svasammukhīnaḥ sadā sannihitaś ca.* ***ayaṃ*** *svānubhavasamasamayam eva sākṣātkṛtaḥ*).
>
> "This you,—this means that the ultimate reality is 'I'. Like those on the shore [of a river] (*vāra*)[2] think of their side as 'this side' (*vāra*) and the other side as 'that side' *pāra*, in the same way those standing on the other side think of their side as the 'this side' *vāra* and the other side as 'that side' *pāra*. Like one and the same man is the son of his father, the father of his son [...]—in this way, even though consisting of such connections (reality) is only one. In this way it is proven that the words 'you' and 'I' are mutual synonyms." (*tvam ayam ity anenāham iti paramārthaḥ. yathā vārasthāḥ vāraṃ vāraṃ pāraṃ ca pāraṃ vadanti tat pārasthāś ca teṣāṃ vāraṃ pāraṃ teṣāṃ pāraṃ ca vāraṃ vadanti. yathā caika eva mānavaḥ pituḥ putraḥ putrasya pitā jāmātuḥ śvaśuraḥ śvaśurasya ca jāmātā ity evamādisambandhamayo 'py eka eva. tathā tvam aham iti padayoḥ parasparaparyāyatvaṃ siddhaṃ*).

This doctrine, which is a natural result of the non-dualism pronounced by Sāhib Kaula, is then furnished with proof from a scriptural text: "This is propounded in Vasiṣṭha's treatise on the Yoga with the words 'you, I' [...]" (*etad eva nirṇītaṃ vāsiṣṭhe yoge tvam aham iti śabdābhyām ityādinā*). Presumably[3] the text in question is the *Yogavāsiṣṭha*, referred to here in an unusual way, for in Kashmir this text is known as *Mokṣopāya*.[4]

---

[1] Literally "one's own", or "of the self". [2] The context suggests that *vāra* is here used in the otherwise unattested sense of *avāra*. [3] See below, p. 90, for more details. [4] For the context and history of editions, see Hanneder, *Studies on the Mokṣopāya*.

At this point the author has merely explained the two pronouns at the end of the *mūla*-text. Working his way backward he now gives his interpretation of *paramaśiva*, which—the reader starts to suspect—does not simply mean the "supreme Śiva". Firstly Paramaśiva is analysed as Śiva, who is *para-ma* , who possesses the supreme *mā* [= Lakṣmī], that is the wealth of liberation (*paramaśivaḥ parā mā mokṣalakṣmīr yasya sa paramaḥ*). In similar ways further etymologies are developed, which are supported by Upaniṣadic quotations as well as one line from the so-called *śaivaśruti*, which turns out to be the *Spandakārikā*, and an appropriate quote from the *Śivadṛṣṭi*.

Especially the word *parama* is interpreted in a bewildering number of ways. The *ma* can be derived not only from the noun *mā* in the sense of Lakṣmī, but from the root *mā* in the sense of *pramāti*. The word is thus explained as *paraṃ māti*, in other words *parama* is one who reflects (*pramāti* = *vimṛśati*) the supreme non-dual in himself (*māti pramāti svatantrakartṛtayā svasvarūpābhedamayam etad eva svātmani svātmanā vimṛśatīti saḥ*). Other interpretations start from various analyses of the compound (*paraś cāsau mac ca paramaḥ*), or *ma* is interpreted as a different verb and arrives at "he who removes duality" (*paraṃ dvitīyaṃ minoti prakṣipati dūrīkaroti paramaḥ advitīyaḥ*), and so forth. A detailed analysis of the complete *mūla*-text remains a desideratum. [1]

The Metrical Part

The first, long prose part concludes with the announcement that the author will praise Śiva (*maheśvara*) in the form of his own self and the verses that follow start with this topic of the identity of self and Śiva:

> *namas tubhyaṃ madekāya tvadekāya ca me namaḥ*
> *tubhyaṃ mahyaṃ sadaikasmāy anekasmai namo namaḥ* (1)
>
> Obeisance to you, who are only me and me, who is only you. My obeisance is to you, to me, to him who is always one, who is manifold, obeisance, obeisance.

The verses that follow usually address Śiva in the second person and circle around the topics known from other works of Sāhib Kaula. Here is a selection that may

[1] For some problems connected to this, see below, p. 89ff.

give an impression. Vs. 11 probably contains an allusion to a well-known Upaniṣadic passage,[1] vss. 17–19 contain word plays typical for the author, and show that also on the level of the base text, the author has inserted quite a few *śabdālaṅkāras*.

priyād api priyaḥ prāṇaḥ prāṇasyāpi ya ātmanaḥ
svātmāpi sa kathaṃ nātha vismṛto dhīviloṭhitaḥ (11)

sarvatra sarvadā sārvaḥ sarvataḥ sarvathāpi saḥ
sa eva sa na vevāsi nāsi vāsi na nāsi he (17)

paramas tvaṃ pareṇāpi nāpareṇāpi vā paraḥ
na paro nāparo vāpi svātmanaḥ svātmanāsi saḥ (18)

vyāpya vyāpyam idaṃ vyāptyāpy ativyāptyā tadanyayā
api vyāpakagatyaiva vyāpako vyāpya eva naḥ (19)

One element of style employed regularly by Sāhib Kaula is what poeticians would perhaps classify as apparent paradoxy (*virodhābhāsa*). But in Sāhib Kaula's verses the function is sometimes different: the paradoxical expression is not so much a riddle that can be solved by a different understanding of a grammatical form or a doctrinal detail, as we know from the common usage of the *alaṅkāra*, but the paradox remains. Let us look at the following example:

kathaṃ moho bhavadrūpavihīnaḥ śaṅkarohyate
kathaṃ vā devadeveśa sahitas tena vohyate (23)

How can delusion be determined without your form, o Śaṅkara.
Or else, Lord Śiva,[2] how can it be determined with it?

This is in a sense the good news read from the perspective of the soteriology of Kashmir non-dualist philosophy. Truly there is no delusion, since the world, the content of delusion, is nothing but Śiva: without Śiva, it does not exist, but if it is Śiva, it cannot be delusion.

---

[1] *Bṛhadāraṇyakopaniṣad* 4.5. [2] We find the address of Śiva as *devadeveśa* frequently in the Epos, in Purāṇas and Tantras.

We can, as almost always, find a doctrinal resolution of the paradox: delusion is something effected and removed by Śiva himself. Either Śiva grants us the revelation of his identity as encompassing the world, or he chooses to veil it. But the common notion of delusion, as the author indicates, cannot work, for delusion cannot really be devoid of Śiva's nature, since Śiva effects it. But if it were devoid of Śiva's nature, delusion would be nothing at all. In the end delusion seems to turn out a logical impossibility—if that is what the author wanted to say.

If we do not take this as a *virodhābhāsa*, which is a poetical figure designed to impress the reader with verbal ingenuity, but as a religious text, then there is no need to resolve the contradiction completely. It could well be an expression of the mystery surrounding the appearance of delusion.

There are also verses that more clearly go beyond the normal modes of Śāstric expression:

> *paraṃ vedyaṃ na yasyāsti kuto 'yaṃ paravedakaḥ*
> *vedyavedakatāhīnaṃ śraya ajñam amuṃ vibhum* (59)
>
> Since for him there is nothing else to know, how could he be another (i.e. a separate) knowing subject?[1] You have to resort to this ignorant Lord devoid of object and subject.

I would argue that here Sāhib Kaula stretches the doctrinal boundaries, for it is not common to understand the notion of the absence of subject and object of knowledge as a special type of not-knowing or ignorance. A commentator would be expected to defuse the statement into a mere trope, for instance, a contradiction that is only apparent (*virodhābhāsa*), for God only appears to be ignorant, but is in reality omniscient. But there is no reason why a particular type of scholastics should have the last word in interpreting an author who so obviously delights in uncommon expressions.

Here Sāhib Kaula's individual terminology reminds one of the anonymous 14th century Christian mystic, who taught that god is separated from man by a "cloude of vnknowyng" and that it is by entering this cloud that one can find the divine.[2]

> *nivartate nijān naiva pañcakṛtyamayāt kṛtāt*
> *yo na kartāpi karteva sa jayaty eka īśvaraḥ* (62)

[1] The option to understand *para* as "higher" does not make much sense. [2] See Hodgson, *The Cloud of Unknowing and the Book of Privy Counselling*, p. 23.

This verse fuses the philosophical and theological worlds Sāhib Kaula is working in. The first line is an adaptation of a Śaiva idea—Pāda a quotes *Spandakārikā*—, but in the second half this is joined to the idea that he is not really an agent, but only appears as one. This phrase is frequently found in Vedāntic sources.

In verses 248–254 we find a treatment of the seven states of the perceiving subject in a very specifically doctrinal Śaiva manner that is not very frequently encountered in the author's work. The passage ends with verse 276 and then follows a prose passage that concludes the whole text.

To sum up: The text is a medley of philosophical and religious doctrines, presented in the manner of ornate Kāvya prose as well as verses with complicated and ambiguous word divisions, and often can not easily be reduced to a single layer of meaning. In the auto-commentary Sāhib Kaula has indicated that he sees an inordinately large numer of meanings at play. We might argue that this—at least for the author—is not a normal linear text, but one that stretches the limits of meaning, and the reader of the manuscript version of the *Kalpavṛkṣa* will have rightly wondered why on earth the author did this to a text of basically Śāstric content. The answer, of course, is that this is not a normal text.

The Intexts

While some problems of this text with its enigmatic intexts could be solved, no meaningful rationale for the selection of Sanskrit quotations contained in the paratexts could be found, and too many remained completely unintelligible. Furthermore the title seemed to indicate that the text, or more specifically the cloth version, should resemble a *Kalpavṛkṣa*. But in which way? A tree fulfilling wishes, perhaps, but which ones specifically? Were the red lines intended to represent graphically the "wish-fulfilling tree"? First I could not see how. A larger reproduction of the cloth afforded the occasion to discuss the pattern with colleagues and visitors, which resulted in fascinating new approaches—like that for instance it might present a schematic map—but none of these theories could be corroborated.

What if the title was just a metaphor for the base text yielding intexts? But the magical "tree" did not seem to present the reader with spectacular texts, these were mostly run-of-the-mill quotations with no inner coherence: the Gāyatrī-mantra, the beginning of the *Kumārasambhava*, and so on.

The auto-commentary, which is available just for the beginning, is of course helpful for interpreting the *mūla*-text, but at the same time it is aggravating the problem by giving a large number of apparently simultaneously valid interpretations. Even innocuous words, like *parama* in *parameśvara*, are reinterpreted in as many ways as grammar and etymology stretched to its limits permit. As the cloth with its literary puzzle, this commentary is something in between a Śāstric commentary and a piece of verbal art. But there is not the slightest indication of the intexts.

Before dealing with more details, let me remind the reader that the aesthetic effect cannot be captured by reproducing parts of it in a book, nor by an illegibly

small view of the whole. The small writing on the large cloth meant that one had to stand fairly near to the object in order to be able to read it. By reading larger sections and then stepping back and viewing the whole, one could start to discover its secrets and admire the author's ingenuity.

The Sources

From the manuscripts of the *mūla*-text mentioned above a reader could not infer that the text was intended to be written onto a large cloth and that by doing so it would reveal a large number of intexts. In a sense only the cloth versions contain the full text, the mūla-manuscripts are just abstracts.

Three such cloths are deposited in the *Oriental Research Library* in Srinagar and were scanned by the *National Mission for Manuscripts.* All transmit the base text with comparatively minor variation and differ mainly in scribal invocations and colophons. The outer appearance suggests that all go back to one single exemplar, probably Sāhib Kaula's 17th century original. In the following those scribal additions are mentioned that have a bearing on the history of the text. All observations are made on the basis of scans.

The Old Cloth (C_1)

Manuscript 8747 (C_1) in the Oriental Research Library, Srinagar, is likely the oldest of the cloth versions. It is written on a coarsely woven fabric and the script is partly fading. The text is written in a very legible Śāradā hand. Furthermore there is a colophon that mentions as scribe Gaṇeśa Kaula:

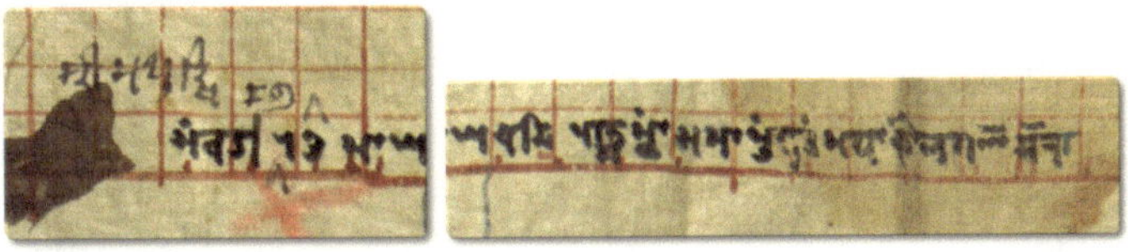

saṃvat 53 māgha vadi pañcamyāṃ samāptaṃ †taṃ mayā kaula-gaṇeśena

A small hand in scrawly script adds *saptarṣi 49,* which can neither be reconciled with śaka 53, nor with vikramasaṃvat 53.

If we can identify Gaṇeśa Kaula as Gaṇeśa (Bhaṭṭāraka), a pupil of Sāhib Kaula, we could interpret the date as *vikramasaṃvat* 1753, i.e. 1697 A.D. This is, however, a wild guess, since the name is not unique enough and it is difficult to say whether the state of preservation of the fabric tallies with this assumption.

The 19th century Śāradā Cloth (C_2)

Manuscript 2190 in the Oriental Research Library, Srinagar, has a little more information on the scribe and date. In the upper left corner we find the following scribal statement:

> *śrīgaṇādhipataye namaḥ / śrīdevyai sadā suphaladāyinyai namo namaḥ / śrīsāhibakaulapādā vijayantāṃtarām om /*
>
> *oṃ namaḥ śivāya / oṃ namo nārāyaṇāya // oṃ namognibhuve / oṃ namas sūryāya / śrīr astu sadā me /*
>
> *śrīgurave śivāyoṃ namo namaḥ śrīmacchrīsāhibaśrīmadvidyādhara-kaulebhyo namo namaḥ*

What this means is that the writer is mentioning his teacher Vidyādhara Kaula, a name that comes up in a manuscript of the *Śyāmāpaddhati* of Sāhib Kaula, where Vidyādhara seems to have been the Guru of the scribe in the lineage prayer.[1]

At the end of the text there is an additional scribal colophon centred on the cloth, in which it is stated that the manuscript was written by Mukunda Kaula, disciple of Vidyādhara Kaula during the reign of Ranbir Singh, to be exact in the year 46 (A.D. 1870):

> *kāśmīrān paritaḥ praśāsati sati śrīraṇavīre nṛpe śāke ṣaṭchruti-sammite haratithau daivejyavāre śubhe śrīmatkaulamukundas sakalavicchrīnāthavidyādharaprāptabuddhimahāśayolikhadimaṃ śrīkalpavṛkṣāgamam //*

The Nāgarī Cloth (C_3)

Manuscript 2189 in the Oriental Research Library, Srinagar, can be also dated to the second half of the nineteenth century, both by appearance and by the fact that

[1] See Hanneder, *To edit or not to edit*, p. 262.

the introduction of the Devanāgarī script to the region on a wider scale can be dated to the Dogras and specifically to the reign of Ranbir Singh. The style of writing with a broader reed pen, and the more rectangular look of the Kashmirian Nāgarī style, gives this cloth a very different feel from the Śāradā ones. Most images in the following pages are from this manuscript, simply for the reason that many interested readers may not be very familiar with the Śāradā script.

Some Examples for Intexts

If we put ourselves into the position of a contemporary reader, it becomes obvious that the cloth is too large to be viewed in toto and read. One either has to step near to be able to decipher the comparatively small script, or step back to have an overview. A reader will probably inspect the cloth starting from the left upper corner, where the base text begins, and the persevering reader will notice that this is a continuous and fairly long text.

At first glance the text written in red—which starts in the first square—suggests to the reader other directions of reading, and here one encounters the main feature

of the text: that it can often be read in more than one way. It seems that the author wanted to guide the viewer to understand the principle and be able to explore the cloth.

The very beginning of the text, the word *śrīmat*, can in fact be read as part of three distinct texts: (a) the base text from left to right, which gives the beginning of the text as known from the manuscripts (*śrīmacchrīsvasvatantrānāśrita* [...]). Then there are two ways to start with the first squares but read downwards. One option (b) is to take the first two akṣaras per line and progress downwards. The resulting text turns out to be a kind of introduction of the author and the work in the *anuṣṭubh* metre:

> *śrīmanmāheśvarācāryavaryacaryātiviśrutaḥ*
> *jayati svānubhūtisthaḥ kalpavṛkṣaphalo guruḥ*

The third option (c) is to follow another red line by going right three squares, then down and up again resulting in: *śrīmacchrīnāthakaulakaḥ sarājakaulakānujaś ciraṃ jīvati jayati ca.*[1] The part of the cloth given above contains just a part of the relevant section.

If we continue text (b) downwards—it runs almost to the bottom of the cloth—, we find a medley of standard quotations and two from Utpaladeva's *Kārikās*, a mixture between Advaita Vedānta and Pratyabhijñā quite typical of our author:

***Bhagavadgītā* 2.21** *na jāyate mriyate vā kadācin nāyaṃ bhūtvā bhavitā vā na bhūyaḥ ajo nityaḥ śāśvato 'yaṃ purāṇo na hanyate hanyamāne śarīre*

***Bhagavadgītā* 10.8** *ahaṃ sarvasya prabhavo mattaḥ sarvaṃ pravartate*

***Bhagavadgītā* 7.7** *mayi sarvam idaṃ protaṃ sūtre maṇigaṇā iva*

***Dakṣiṇamūrtistotra* 1a** *viśvaṃ darpaṇadṛśyamānanagarītulyaṃ nijāntargataṃ*

(source unclear) *tad eko vaśiṣṭhaḥ śivaḥ kevalo 'haṃ*

***Anuttarāṣṭika* 1a:** *saṃkrāmo na na bhāvanā na ca kathāyuktir na carcā na ca*

***Īśvarapratyabhijñākārikā* 1.1** *kathaṃcid āsādya maheśvarasya*

***Chāndogyopaniṣad* 3.14.1** *sarvaṃ khalv idaṃ brahma*

***Bṛhadāraṇyakopaniṣad* 4.4.19** *neha nānāsti kiñcana*

Kaṭhopaniṣad *mṛtyos sa mṛtyum āpnoti ya iha nāneva paśyati*

[1] The word Śrīnātha is too unspecific to be decoded into a proper name.

Taittirīyopaniṣad **2.4.1** *yato vāco nivartante aprāpya manasā saha ānandaṃ brahmaṇo vidvān na bibhīti*[1] *kutaścana*

Śivastotrāvalī **20.11** *bhaktilakṣmīsamṛddhānāṃ kim anyad upayācitaṃ enayā vā daridrāṇāṃ kim anyad upayācitaṃ*

Śvetāśvataropaniṣad **3.15** *yad bhūtaṃ yac ca bhavyam*

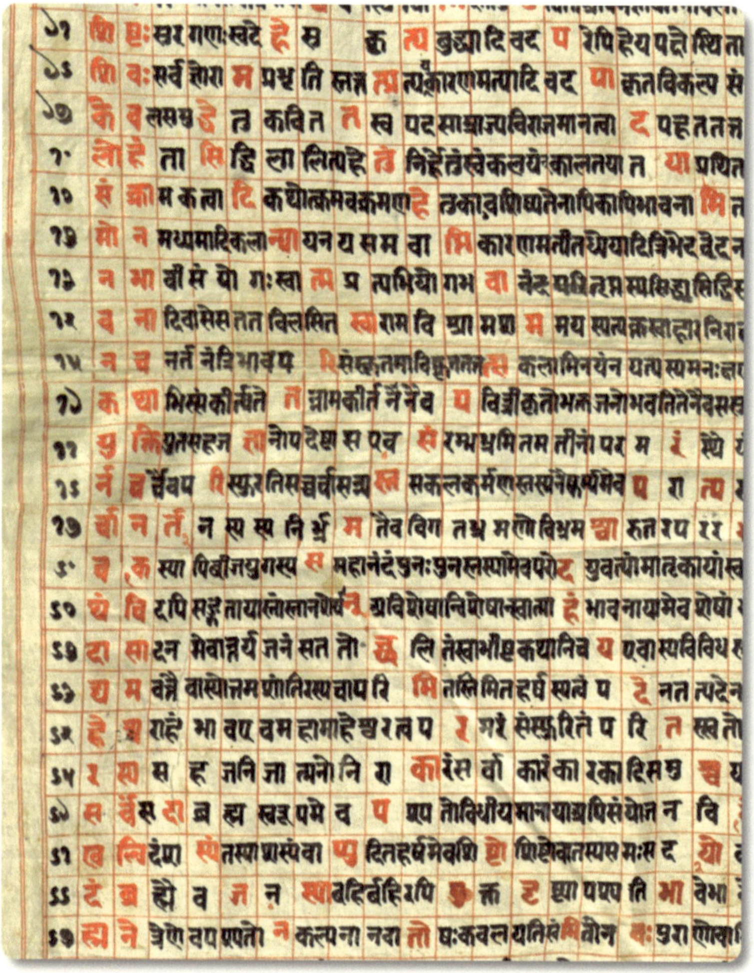

[1] Since Kashmirian pronunciation does not properly distinguish *ī* from *e*, *bibhīti* is here understood as *bibheti*.

In the cloth we find that quotations often remain incomplete and are merely of the beginning of a text, but the quotation of the first *Īśvarapratyabhijñākārikā* seems to stop a bit too abruptly with *kathaṃcid āsādya maheśvarasya.* But in fact the verse is continued further to the right, which encourages the reader to discover yet another way to read texts in this puzzle. One has to read *ka* in 80.2 (i.e. line 80, row 2), then jump down (81.1–2) to *thaṃcid* and continue down to *maheśvarasya*, but then move down diagonally where we find the rest of the first kārikā with *dāsyaṃ* continuing zigzag upwards in a line too long to reproduce in book size.

> *kathaṃcid āsādya maheśvarasya dāsyaṃ janyasyāpy upakāram icchan*
> ...

But this is not the only instance, where our tree, as it were, branches out: The *ka* in 80.2 is marked with a small digit "1", which is an indication of a further way to read. And indeed, following diagonally upward we can read *kartari jñātari svātmany ādisiddhe* [...], which turns out to be the second of Utpaladeva's *Kārikās*.

This first example may have given the impression that it was the intention of the author to place one akṣara per square: obviously the red texts are always written with only one akṣara per square and also the first rows of text start in such an orderly fashion. But a closer look reveals that the principle is quite often violated. Sometimes more text is squeezed in, at other times the scribe was saving too much space first and later had to leave a field empty. The example on the right is from the right end of the cloth—here it is the Śāradā version C_2—, where we find too much text between the two red vertical lines, but not enough to fill all the lines. Examples continue throughout the text, and the phenomenon is almost identical on all three cloth versions. There is also a tendency to read more text between the red lines further down the cloth, which results in the lower half appearing significantly darker than the upper half. As we shall see, the scribes must have known what was supposed to stand in the squares with red intexts and were thus unlikely to produce any errors there. It is also clear from the above example that there is no easy way to improve the layout of the text: in line 33 the scribe had to squeeze double lines

with nine akṣaras between the red text, but shifting the red line further right would have created more problems than it could solve, for line 42 has used up all squares.

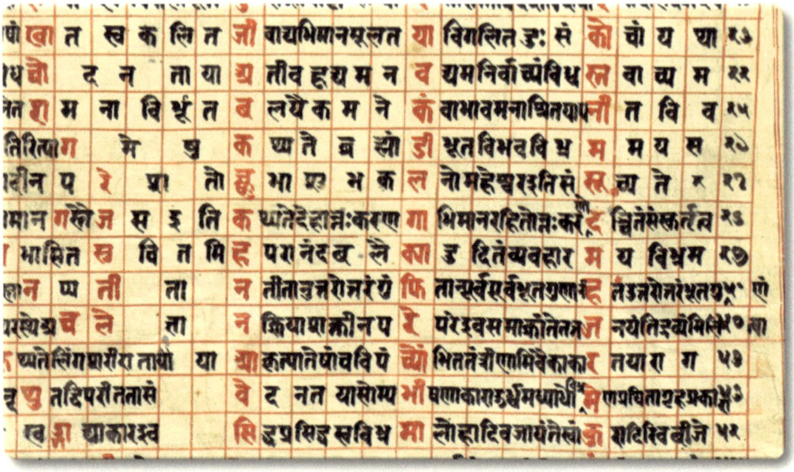

If we finally look at the Nāgarī version, we can see that every scribe had his own problems of filling in the text on the right side.

This problem and the different solutions bring into focus the question of how the cloths were written, that is, how the author composed and wrote the first version, but also how it was reproduced later.

What is most spectacular in this puzzle is that a seemingly normal text, the base text of the *Kalpavṛkṣa*, is at the same time the source of a larger number of additional intexts, if only written in the right manner. So while the reader is supposed to wonder about the inscrutable transformation from base to intext, I think the obvious solution is that the author started the composition with the intexts. Perhaps an author of superior mental capacities would have been able to devise the base text while continuously calculating the positions of the red akṣaras with mathematical precision to form the multitude of intexts. But if he had done so—the fact that text between red lines had to be stretched or squeezed in is already a compelling counter-argument—he would have failed to intuit a much easier method, which I think is the most likely answer to the question, of how the cloth was produced. The author must have started by writing the red texts directly on the cloth in the

first step, and only then composed the base text to be filled in. Then the first cloth would have to be considered the original.

But let us continue with some more examples. Another natural centre of attention is in the middle of the whole cloth, where we find a square of eight by eight, with red texts going into the four directions.

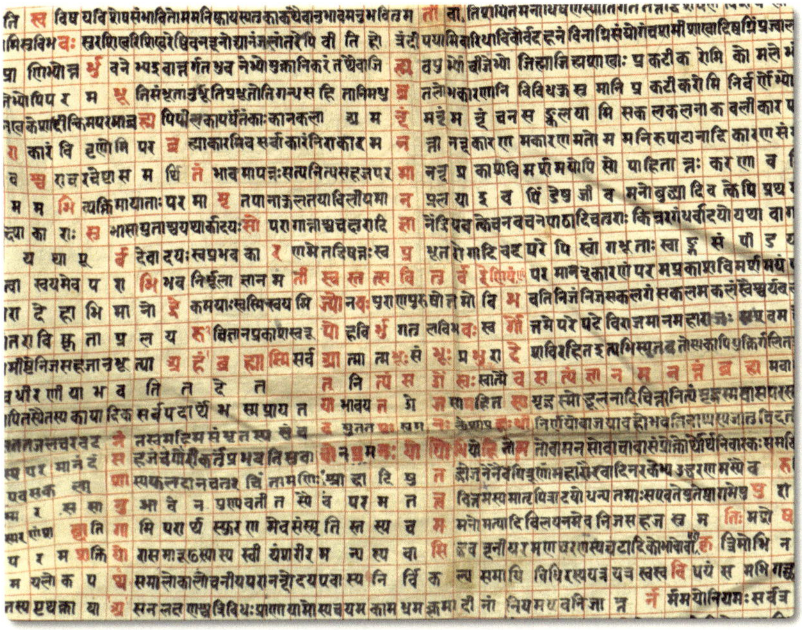

Starting in the upper left corner and going clockwise around the square we can read the Gāyatrī mantra. From the square upward, we read *prajñānam ānandaṃ brahma*, to the right *satyaṃ jñānam anantaṃ brahma*, downward *tat tvam asi*, from the left: *ahaṃ brahmāsmi*, in the square *oṃ bhūr bhuvaḥ svaḥ*, and going diagonally up left we have *jyotīrasomṛtaṃ brahma* [...]

If one continues reading, one notices that much ingenuity was applied to producing different text shapes, there are lines going in all directions, squares, and there is also one rhombic shaped text:

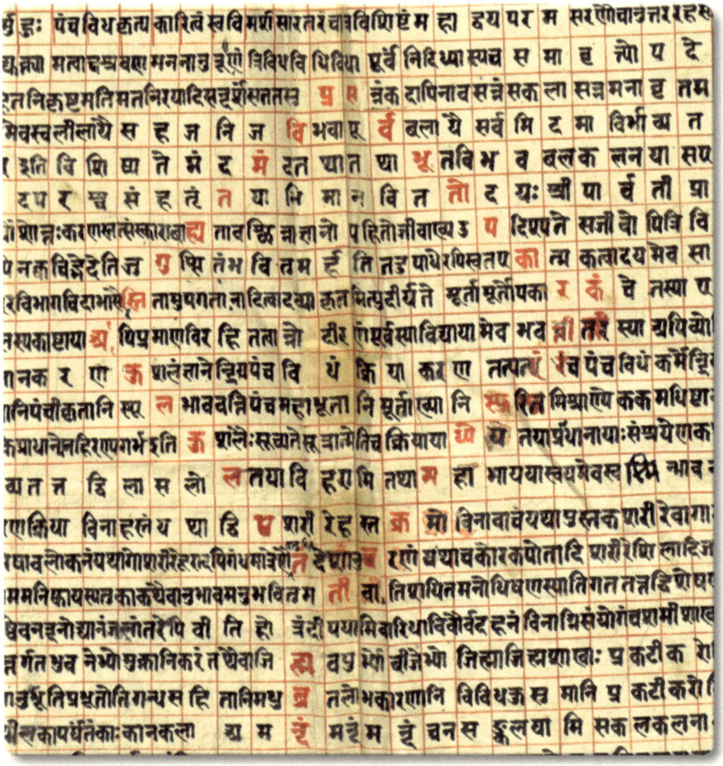

Here the text starts in the left corner and reads, in the upper half, the first line of *Devīmāhātmya* 2.2:

> *asti guhyatamaṃ vipra sarvabhūtopakārakaṃ*

But there are two digits "1" in the square containing the initial "*a*", so it is worth trying to read counter-clockwise for the rest. Here we read:

> *akulakulapatantī cakramadhye sphurantī*

The rest is difficult to make sense of, and it is unclear where the text continues.

The cloth contains a wide variety of shapes and variations. Here is one example that adds a further dimension by bringing in philosophical content. It is a rather simple structure consisting of two texts progressing in different directions, which

merely share the first akṣara *a*—with the usual small indicatory numbers alerting to the fact that this akṣara starts more than one text. One text is to be read upwards, where it yields *atha yogānuśāsanam,* the other downwards as *athāto brahmajijñāsā.* This may be a simple enough play on words, but one that implies an interesting syncretistic image: both systems, Yoga and Vedānta, here represented through the initial Sūtras of their respective foundational texts, both proceed, as it were, from the same starting point.

In the next example Sāhib Kaula writes a verse in red simply from left to right so that it coincides with the base text, which reads: *yasmin sarvaṃ yataḥ sarvaṃ cetyādiśāstranirūpitanisarga-* [...] The passage in red is *yasmin sarvaṃ yataḥ sarvaṃ,* which is as indicated by the author a quotation, namely of *Mahābhārata* 12.47.54. If we follow the red text, we find the full quotation of the śloka from the *Mahābhārata.*

> *yasmin sarvaṃ yatas sarvaṃ yat sarvaṃ sarvataś ca yat*
> *yaś ca sarvamayo nityaṃ tasmai sarvātmane namaḥ*

Here the main feature lies in the relation between the base and the intext, the latter being a sort of footnote to the base text, which provides the complete verse that is cited only with its first pāda in the base text.

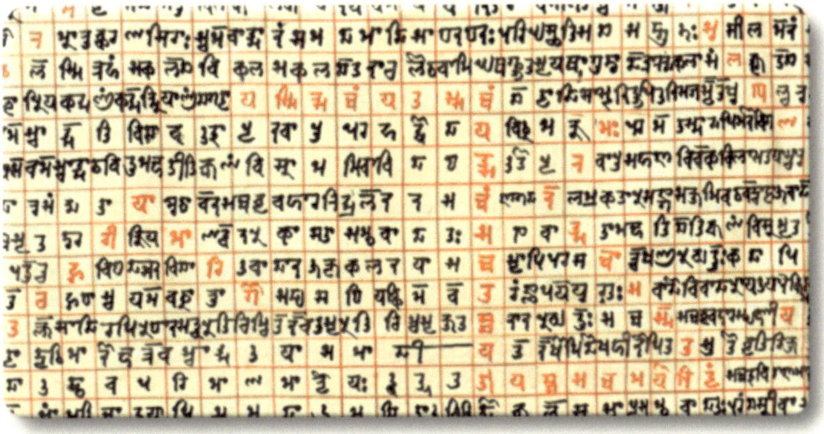

As stated above, small numbers in the cloths occasionally indicate the direction of reading: the start, that is, the first akṣara, is marked with a "1", the next akṣara

with a "2", which gives the initial direction and sometimes alerts the reader to the fact that more than one reading direction is possible. One rather intricate example for this is the following passage.

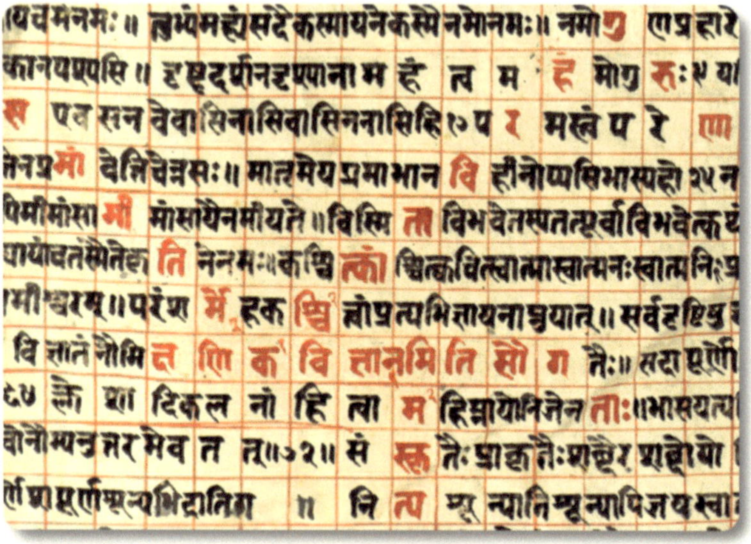

In this intersections of texts, the syllable *ka*, which is marked with the digit "1" in the upper right corner of the square, is part of four texts, and the *na* in *vijñānam* can also be read downwards. Of course, only the beginning of the texts, which spread out in all directions in various shapes, could be reproduced here.[1]

1. *kṣaṇi**ka**vijñānam iti saugatāḥ*. This can be counted twice, since it is part of the base text (with *saugatāḥ*), but also marked in red as an intext.
2. ***ka**rmeti mīmāṃsakāḥ*.
3. ***ka**ścit kāntāvirahaguruṇā* [...] Here then follows the first stanza of the *Meghadūta*.
4. *namaskṛtya parāṃ vācaṃ devīṃ trividhavigraham* (*Alaṃkārasarvasva* 1). This text runs downward from the *na* in *vijñānam*.

[1] On the left side another scan would have to be fitted to the fragment reproduced, which leads to unpleasent optical distortions.

Although much could be said about the details that the viewer was supposed to discover,[1] when viewing the cloth, this discovery of the intexts presents no fundamental difficulties, since the rubrication serves as an infallible guide. The text does not constitute as much a riddle one has to solve, rather a structure one can only slowly discover and appreciate the ingenuity behind its construction. Unfortunately this does not fully apply when one has to use scans of segments that constituted one sixth of the whole and were too warped to be simply fit together, that was the state with which our research had to content itself.

[1] The critical editor reading all three preserved cloths would of course notice that some details are executed with more precision in one or the other cloth. I have ignored these types of variants, since even their explanation would presuppose that one has all three sources in front of oneself.

Other Intexts in Sanskrit

A selection of further intexts in Sanskrit is given here in tabular form, but the list is not complete. Some texts are either too small, or cannot be properly connected and read in the intended sequence. Where more than one text begins in the same place, in other words, when one square is the starting point of different intexts to be read in different directions, these texts are distinguished by prefixing (a), (b), etc. to them.

[35.43]	sāhibkaularaseśvaro vijayate śāntātmatābhāsvaraḥ
[9.70]	śṛṅgārī svamatau hasajjanagatiṃ bhakteṣu kāruṇyavān
[15.19]	ekasmai kṛtyakṛtyāya nityāya vimalātmane nirvikalpacidākhyāya mahyam eva namo namaḥ
[37.28]	śivaḥ śaktyā yukto yadi bhavati śakto prabhavituṃ (*Saundaryalaharī* 1)
[59.18]	caitanyam ātmā (*Śivasūtra* 1.1)
[52.33]	sa nityopalabdhisvarūpo ātmā (*Hastāmalakastotra*) 12
[86.19]	yo yo bhāvaḥ svāmidṛṣṭo yuto vā saumyair vā syāt tasya tasya vṛddhiḥ (?)
[92.29]	(a) aham evāsam evāgre nānyad yat sadasat paraṃ (b) asty uttarasyāṃ diśi devatātmā (*Kumārasambhava* 1.1)
[78.17]	paścād ahaṃ yad etac ca yo 'vaśiṣyeta so 'smy ahaṃ (*Bhāgavatapurāṇa* 2.9.32)
[101.–]	(a) vāgarthāv iva saṃpṛktau (*Raghuvaṃśa* 1.1) (b) vāsudevaḥ sarvam iti (*Bhagavadgītā* 7.19)
[86.81]	(a) pramāṇādiṣoḍaśapadārthānāṃ tattvajñānān niśśreyasādhigamaḥ (*Nyāyasūtra* 1) (b) prajāpatim evāpy abruyuḥ
[100.99]	(a) śriyaḥ patiḥ śrīmati śāsituṃ jagat (*Śiśupālavadha* 1.1) (b) śriyaḥ kurūṇām adhipasya pālanīṃ (*Kirātārjunīya* 1.1)
[11. 85]	gaṇānāṃ tvā gaṇapatiṃ havāmahe (*Ṛgveda* 2.23.1)
[15.19]	ekasmai kṛtyakṛtyāya nityāya vimalātmane (*Mokṣopāya* 5.80.40)
[56.44]	mahimna pāraṃ te paramaviduṣo yadyasadṛśī (*Śivamahimnaḥstotra* 1)

[11.101] śriyaṃ devīm upa hvaye śrīr mā devī juṣatām. (This quotation, the first part of which is *Ṛgvedakhila* 5.87.3c, is contained in ritual texts from different traditions.)

[106.61] jīyāt kṛtānaṅgapataṅgadāhaḥ (*Śrīkaṇṭhacarita* 1.1)

Obviously we find here the beginnings of many texts, or else the most important quotations from them.

The Colophon of the *Kalpavṛkṣa*

The primary colophon of the *Kalpavṛkṣa*, which is transmitted in all sources, cloths as well as complete manuscripts, turns out to be a mine of information:

> *ity evam ayaṃ* ***śrīkalpapādapapatibandho*** *bandhanābandhanabandhanapratibandhanapratipādanadhanamahādvayādisudarśanasudarśanasudarśanaḥ kaśyapamahāmuniviracitāpūrvapūrvaracanasarvadeśaviśeṣaśeṣasatīsarovarāparākāraṇakaśmīradeśakṛtasannidhānasvasvātantryamahomahimasvīkṛtaśrīmacchrī****sāhibkaulā****bhidhānopavanakṛtaparamavimalaśivāspadena na kenāpi kenāpi nirekena nirekena kena kenacid* ***viracitasumanodalaphalaśākhāskandādiparamāracanasuracanaḥ*** *śrīmacchrīmaruvāṭadeśaviśeṣādhipati paramajñānamūrtivigalitāsārasaṃsārāpārāvārāvārasmṛtimahārājādhirājacakravartipati****yaśovatsiṃhā****bhidhānamahārāja****pranunnena mayā*** *satāṃ paramakāruṇyavatāṃ mumukṣāvatāṃ ca suphalabalalālityāya cākamītutamām iti* //

The style is complex as usual, but if we simplify the construction, we arrive at:

> "Thus (*ity evam*) this wish-fulfilling tree on a cloth[1] composed (*viracita*) with flowers, leaves, fruits, branches and stem, by me (*mayā*) whose supreme pure state of Śiva (*paramavimalaśivāspadena*) is in the garden called *sāhibkaula*, instigated by Yaśovatsiṃha […]

[1] *pati* for *paṭi*?

If this interpretation is correct, this would be a colophon to the visual *Kalpavṛkṣa* by the author Sāhib Kaula himself. The colophon continues with the date of completion of the work following all kinds of calculation methods, which will be discussed in my forthcoming edition of Sāhib Kaula's works.

The Wish-fullfilling Tree of Languages

The final part of the riddle concerning the text and its visual representation was solved only through reexamining the 1327-page codex Hs. or. 12509 (Staatsbibliothek Berlin, Preußischer Kulturbesitz), which contained materials connected to Sāhib Kaula. What we have ignored so far is the fact that many intexts are not in Sanskrit. Some are obviously in Indian vernaculars, others remained undecipherable at first. It was easy to suspect these texts to be in one or even more languages, but in the complicated state of transmission it was difficult—at least for a mere Sanskritist—to find out more. The Berlin manuscript contains a key to this puzzle: it lists, on a few pages reproduced and transcribed below, the non-Sanskritic intexts and adds either the literary source or the language!

The first surprise was the sheer number of languages listed, which is thirty-six. The second was their geographical distribution: While Hindustani or Panjabi are more or less to be expected, also Gujarati and perhaps Bengali, the inclusion of Persian is unusual. Not from the perspective of actual distribution and usage at the time, but from the perspective of its representation in Śāstric and religious texts. Furthermore the inclusion and naming of examples from South-Indian languages (*drāviḍabhāṣā*) in a Kashmirian environment is noteworthy.

Unfortunately quite a few specimina of languages cannot be accounted for. Probably some of the attempts to transcribe fairly remote languages did not succeed. In some cases the incompatibilies with Kashmirian pronunciation may alone be the reason, in others, informants may perhaps have exaggerated their abilities. For that reason I would refrain from making any pronouncements as to which quotes are faulty or even fake, for a highly deficient transcription alone may render

a language—even one that the reader knows—quite incomprehensible.[1] Furthermore to expect that all problems of transcription of Indian languages had been already solved in the seventeenth-century Kashmir may be unrealistic.

Some of the quotes are indentifiable if we allow for some variation:[2] *merāmojyamaiṃ kachyunahīṃ* [...] is by Kabir and more familiar today as *merā mujha meṃ kucha nahīṃ* [...], the name *soradāsa* should refer to Sūrdās, and the identification *vaṅgadeśakisodāsasya* should denote the Bengali poet Kṛṣṇadāsa, but the quotation cannot be transformed into meaningful Bengali.

The problems are compounded by some unclear names of languages. The intext quote *mahārājyajasvanta-jyī ko jyai hove*—see below on the context of this line—is described as *mūluānībhāṣā*. Here Malvānī comes to mind, but one would expect that, since the author mentions the ruler of Marwar here, it should be in the language of Marwar, rather than a Koṅkani dialect. Is Siṅrī to be interpreted as Sindhī? Or take the case of the *bhuḍḍhadeśa-bhāṣā*, which might be a bowdlerised *bhoṭadeśabhāṣā*, but the actual quotation, which from a Kashmirian perspective could be in Ladakhi, remains undecipherable.[3] From this backgroud it is interesting to note that one of the examples in the most unexpected language, which is Arabic, is actually meaningful and perfectly understandable.[4] In the Berlin manuscript we read this passage as *koleśayanmuhīt*, which is identified as *arabhī-bhāṣā*.[5] Interestingly the cloths have a slightly different transcription. As seen in the image, the Nāgarī cloth reads *kollośayīnmuhīt*,[6] as do the other cloths. The Arabic phrase, in proper transcription *kullu šai'in muḥīṭ*, means "all-encompassing".[7]

The Persian quote (*pārisīkabhāṣā*), too, can be made sense of. It runs as *khāna ālama hameṣāṃbarkhurdār*[8] *bhāṣad*, and is a transcription of the Persian *ḫān-i*

[1] Even a seasoned Sanskritist may not be able to intuit the Sanskrit word behind *eteron*, Friedrich Schlegel's transciption of skt. *itaram*! [2] For the following I am indebted to Hans Harder. [3] *atadamuyutha* || *amudamuyutha* || *yuthayutha* || [4] For the identification I am indebted to my colleague Oliver Kahl. [5] See the facsimile with transcript below, p. 86. [6] Please note that the final *t* in the Śāradā manuscripts is not written as a ligature, but as a full akṣara with the *sa* added to it, as if applied later. [7] Literally "everything is contained in it". [8] *khur* is in fact missing in the Berlin manuscript, but contained in all cloths.

ʿālam hamīša ʿām-barḫurdār bāšad.[1] Here we find some variation in the sources, and this is of course what we would expect in view of the varying transcription of foreign languages into a Sanskrit environment in Kashmir.

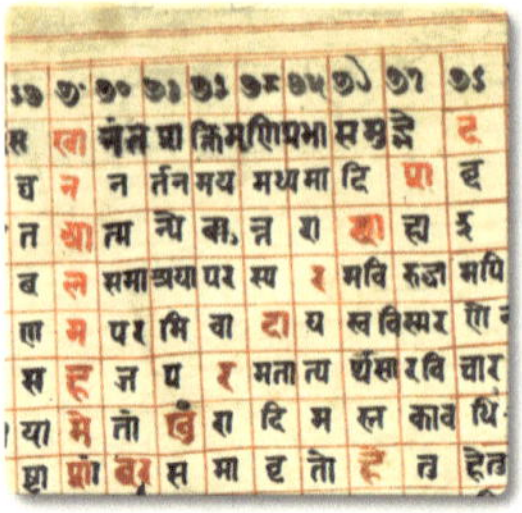

Although the text is the same, we see that the older cloth on the right (C_1) is more exact. In the *śāṃ* the left cloth (C_3) has written the vowel and the anusvāra in black, and in the middle example (C_2) the *khu* is not in a square, but squeezed in between. The *khu* also has a dot on top like an anusvāra, which is wrong, since the base text reads *khurādi.*

The Language of the Author

Identifying the languages of the non-Sanskritic intexts, which is beyond the competence of the present author, may take more time, but there is one quotation important for our view of the author:

> *jyuyīṣāsoyībhayā* || *ṣānathātu ānanda chyayā* || *nisadina anubhava-bhāḍenayānayā āp bhayātu kahāṃ bhayā* ||
> *iyaṃ granthakartuḥ svakīyabhāṣā*
>
> Variants:
> C_3: *joyīthāsoyībhayā thānathātu ānanda cchayā nisadina anubhava-bāḍenayā nayā āpa bhayātu kahā bhayā*
> C_2: *joyīthāsoyībhayā thānathātu ānanda cchayā anubhavabāḍenayā*

This passage is identified in the Berlin manuscript[2] as being in the "own language of the author".[3] This may come as a surprise, for the text is not even in a dardic

[1] I am grateful to Anna Martin for the identification. [2] See below, p. 81. [3] The following is based on an analysis kindly provided by Monika Horstmann.

language, and thus it appears that Sāhib Kaula's own tongue, meaning perhaps the language of his family, was not Kashmirian.

The implication of this finding is slightly more complicated. Some time ago Sanderson has formulated the theory that the Kaulas were immigrants from Mithila,[1] based on several arguments. One was the rather specific note by the scribe Dīlārāma Kaula stating that his family ancestry lies in Mithila.[2] Another corroborating fact was the "eastern" pantheon of deities that is mentioned in texts by the Kaulas, as well as their non-Kashmirian Gotra.

However, the quotation above does not point to Mithila. There are several conceivable solutions of the problem: perhaps Dīlārāma immigrated from another place than Sāhib Kaula, the Berlin manuscript's identification could be wrong, or the Kaulas were originally Maithila Brahmins, but long living abroad and speaking another language before moving to Kashmir. Whatever the explanation, the case needs to be reevaluated.

Classifying the *Kalpavṛkṣa*

So far I have tried to avoid discussing the theory of visual poetry and describe the *Kalpavṛkṣa* as a stand-alone piece to be understood without much external information on the genre. There is some justification for doing this, for it is how contemporary readers or viewers had to approach it.

But stating that the *Kalpavṛkṣa* is a specimen of visual poetry and that it can be described as part of the widely attested practice of combining visual and literary art—thus the perhaps least complicated definition of the genre—means opening two cans of worms. The first problem lies in the classification of visual poetry in the indigenous framework of *citrakāvya*, the second concerns the European taxonomy of visual poetry. Neither topic is without its own problems, but the main complication is that, strangely enough, the *Kalpavṛkṣa* fits the second much better than the first.

---

[1] See Sanderson, "The Śaiva Religion among the Khmers," p. 362. [2] For this, including a reproduction of the folio, see Hanneder, "Pre-modern Sanskrit Authors, Editors and Readers," p. 234–237.

The *Kalpavṛkṣa* as *citrakāvya*

If one were to translate the term "visual poetry" into Sanskrit, one would probably arrive at the word *citrakāvya,* the very term used for a type of classical Indian poetry. This parallelism in terminology as well as the fact that both European and Indian ornate literature use palindroms, acrostics and other comparable techniques is an interesting avenue for comparison, one that has been explored by focussing on international, but pre-modern examples by Ernst [1] and in a highly comprehensive manner by Dencker. [2]

But the comparative angle has also been a source of confusion, for most Indian visual poetry differs in a crucial way from European specimina in being still predominantly oral literature. The point has been made by all Indological authors, but its implications have sometimes been kept in the background for the sake of comparison, but in our case this point is important for explaining what the *Kalpavṛkṣa* is.

Just as in the case of visual poetry in Europe there is a controversy in India about whether *citrakāvya* is good poetry. Every reader of Sanskrit poetry knows that simpler embellishments are virtually omnipresent. However, the term *citrakāvya* often implies that the poet has overdone it, and created a poem, in which some dazzling (*citra*) effect takes precedence over the other poetical qualities. Consequently some Indian poeticians have stated that *citra* is the lowest form of poetry, one that makes up in effects what it is lacking in inspiration. But since with Ānandavardhana, an avowed critic of *citrakāvya,* has written one such poem himself—interpreted sometimes as an aside to critics, who might otherwise argue that his rejection of verbal artistry is only a side-effect of his inability to produce it—the Indian literary scene has remained both ambiguous and fascinated. Some poeticians have explained the varieties in great detail only to state that: "This [the forms of *citra* described in detail] does not acquire the nature of *kāvya,* since it is a poetry that is forced and results merely in word games (*krīḍā*)." [3]

[1] Ernst, *Carmen figuratum: Geschichte des Figurengedichts von den antiken Ursprüngen bis zum Ausgang des Mittelalters.* [2] Dencker, *Optische Poesie. Von den prähistorischen Schriftzeichen bis zu den digitalen Experimenten der Gegenwart.* [3] *The Kāvyānuśāsana of Hemachandra with his own gloss.* Bombay: Nirnaya Sagar Press, reprint New Delhi 1986, p. 272. The word *krīḍā* has a technical meaning, comprising six types of conundrums, but may have been used here in a loose sense.

In modern India, the task to rescue *citrakāvya* from this verdict was carried out by Kalānāth Jhā, the only scholar to have written a monograph on the topic.[1] Only very few other scholars[2] have treated the topic at all and so the literature on visual poetry in India is quite limited.

Kalānāth Jhā also dealt with the interesting issue of visual poetry as a cross-cultural genre. He starts this by saying "Until recently, at least in India, it was believed that citrakāvya was found only there"[3] and continues with a survey of similarities.

Before proceeding with this further, let us review the Indian term *citrakāvya* and its application. Despite appearing on the surface as a literal equivalent of "visual poetry", the word is actually a blanket term for a large variety of verbal artistry—word games, riddles, puzzles, conundrums—and thus much wider than visual poetry. This sense is gained by understanding *citra* not as the noun "image", but as the adjective "striking, dazzling",[4] so that we are not talking of "image (*citra*) poetry" but "dazzling" (*citra*) poetry. In this interpretation the important thing is the technique or aspect through which this effect is accomplished, as, for instance, *śabdacitra* "[poetry] dazzling through sound" or *arthacitra* "[poetry] dazzling through sense". The category of *citra* is therefore quite broad, and can be used for everything from complicated alliterations to large scale *śleṣakāvya*s.[5]

The term figurative poetry used by Kalānāth Jhā in his monograph can thus be misleading. For clarification let us review one of the more elaborate Indian taxonomies, the one given by Bhoja in his *Sarasvatīkaṇṭhābharaṇa*:[6]

---

[1] Jha, *Figurative poetry in Sanskrit literature*. There is also one article by the same author Jha, "Sanskrit Citrakāvyas and the Western Pattern Poem," which is except for the illustrations identical with Jha, "Sanskrit Citrakāvyas and the Western Pattern Poem: A Critical Appraisal." [2] E. g., Lienhard, "Text-Bild-Modelle der klassischen indischen Dichtung" or Vose, "Jain Uses of Citrakāvya and Multiple-Language Hymns in Late Medieval India: Situating the Laghukāvya Hymns of Jinaprabhasūri in the 'Assembly of Poets'." [3] Jha, "Sanskrit Citrakāvyas and the Western Pattern Poem: A Critical Appraisal," p. 109. [4] As expressed in Hemacandra's gloss: *āścaryahetutvād vā citram. The Kāvyānuśāsana of Hemachandra with his own gloss.* Bombay: Nirnaya Sagar Press, reprint New Delhi 1986, p. 257. [5] For an overview see Gerow, *A glossary of Indian figures of speech*, p. 175–189. [6] *The Saraswatī Kaṇṭhābharaṇa by Dhāreshvara Bhojadeva with the Commentary of Rāmsinha (I–III) and Jagaddhara (IV)*. (Kāvyamālā 94). Bombay 1934, p. 265.

> *varṇasthānasvarākāragatibandhān pratīha yaḥ*
> *niyamas tad budhaiḥ ṣodhā citram ity abhidhīyate* (2.109)
>
> The sixfold restriction [1] given by the experts in poetology [2] concerning *varṇa, sthāna, svara, ākāra, gati* and *bandha*, is called *citra.*

The commentators state at the outset that this means that the author does not subscribe to the negative position held by the "Kashmirians", i. e. the *dhvani* school, concerning this type of poetry. [3] Then he makes clear in one brief sentence that one argument for this is that *citra*[*-kāvya*] is not just a combination of text and image, but encompasses much more, [4] since also a restriction of sounds, is called *citra.* [5] This refers, as becomes clear from the example, to verses in which only a certain group of sounds, or even a single consonant is used. The same applies to the next two categories of vowel and place of enunciation. [6]

It is only with the category *ākāra* "form, image" that we reach "poetry dazzling through images", where text is projected into a shape. [7] If we take as another poetician Hemacandra, we can see that he does not enumerate *ākāra* and *bandha* separately, [8] but says that *ākāra* denotes "forms like sword composition and drum composition" (*ākāraḥ khaḍgamurajabandhādyākṛtiḥ*). He then gives examples for both by explaining the verses and giving exact notes where the syllables have to stand in the image. Descriptions like that may be the ultimate sources for the editors' reconstructions of such images. [9]

Bhoja gives as examples lotus designs with varying numbers of petals. Both the old edition of Bhoja's work [10] dating from 1921 and the subsequent Bombay edition have drawings of nineteen *citrabandhas*. Aesthetically in the old edition these drawings look quite different from that of the Kāvyamālā version, reflecting the advances in the craft of book production. The newer ones are more exact, more refined, but also more ornamental.

---

[1] Or: "rule". [2] I understand *iha śāstre.* [3] *citram ālekhyaṃ tad iva jīvitasthānīyadhvanirahitaṃ citram iti kāśmīrakāḥ. tadasat.* ibid. [4] *yad vā ākṛtiviśeṣayuktaṃ citram iti tad api na. avyāpakatvāt.* ibid. [5] *ato varṇādiniyamena pravṛttam āścaryakāritayā citram ity eva yuktam | varṇā vyañjanāni.* ibid. [6] *sthānaṃ kaṇṭhādi. svarā akārādayaḥ.* ibid. [7] *ākāraḥ padmādyākṛtyunmudraṇam.* ibid. [8] *The Kāvyānuśāsana of Hemachandra*, p. 257. [9] *The Kāvyānuśāsana of Hemachandra*, p. 263–265. [10] *Sarasvatīkaṇṭhābharaṇe śrīmadbhojanarendraviracite paricchedatrayaṃ. paṇḍitavaryaratneśvaramiśraviracitayā ratnadarpaṇākhyayā vyākhyayānugataṃ.* [Ed. Drāviḍavireśvara Śāstrī Kāśī vaiśākha sudi 8 bhaume saṃvatsare 1843 [=1921 A.D.]].

The principle behind these *ākāracitras* is always a certain way of reading the text, through which syllables in certain positions are repeated. This is more difficult to explain[1] than to show: in the figure called "lotus" one reads the text of a verse by reading out into all the petals, but returning each time to the centre, thereby repeating the syllable in the centre. Here is one example from Sāhib Kaula himself, for he, too, has produced quite a few traditional *citras* in his *Devīnāmavilāsa*. The fourteenth chapter of this text contains a whole panoply of such figures: *ardhabhrama* (14.1), *tryakṣara* (14.3), *dvyakṣara* 14.85, *ekākṣara* (14.78), *sarvapādayamaka* (14.8), a *cakrabandha* (14.25), *murajabandha* (14.70), and *sarvatobhadra* (14.95). The concluding verse of the chapter contains the typical formula introducing the author, but alerts the reader that this chapter is furnished with "*citraiḥ padyagaṇaiḥ*". In the first verse of the following chapter fifteen there is one more, a lotus composition (*padmabandha*) reproduced here.

In order to read the verse one has to read the syllable in the centre, then read outward to the east, then move to the next petal clockwise and read back from the outside syllable by syllable, then move to the next petal reading outward, but then on the same petal in again, and so forth. It is difficult to know, how much of the additional information in such images is taken from manuscripts or constitutes an editorial addition. In our case the author's note in the concluding verse alerts the reader to the fact that this chapter contains figures, which one might otherwise miss.

The lotus design is ingenious, but it is important to note that neither is the lotus related to the nine-hundred and first name of the goddess (*lalitā*) that forms the topic of the verse, nor is the image specifically formed by the body of the text. The same text could as well be interpreted as the wheel image (*cakra*). In other words the image describes most importantly a patterned or repetitive way of reading, only to some extent a shape into which the text is filled, but it is not an image formed by the text.

---

[1] "When the principle of limitation is not applied to the entire sequence of syllables, but requires repetition only of certain strategically placed syllables in terms of which the whole verse can be arranged in imitation of natural objects [...]." Gerow, *A glossary of Indian figures of speech*, p. 176.

ललिता ॥९०१॥

तारसंप्रथितालोककलोता ललिता तता ।
तातताकलिताभेददभेता हृदि संरता ॥१॥
(पद्मबन्धोऽयम्)

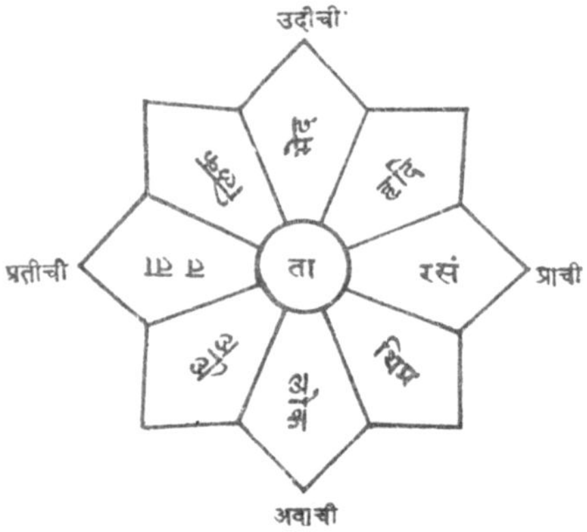

The above reconstruction by the editor is the typical form, in which we encounter the so-called *bandha*s in print. If we look one level below, into the manuscript sources, we find that there are manuscripts, where no attempt is made at a graphical representation, nor any indication that this is *bandha*.[1] And even those who do may differ, as in the following page from a manuscript,[2] which describes the same verse:

[1] The same point is made by Vose with reference to Jinaprabhasūri's works: "Neither the printed texts nor the manuscripts show the verses in the shapes they are meant to take on. This perhaps gives us a clue about how these forms were consumed and enjoyed. Instead of reading them in their shaped patterns on a page, a trained connoisseur would have been challenged to identify the citrabandhas correctly merely by listening for the patterns of syllable repetition in these verses." Vose, "Jain Uses of Citrakāvya and Multiple-Language Hymns in Late Medieval India: Situating the Laghukāvya Hymns of Jinaprabhasūri in the 'Assembly of Poets'," p. 324. [2] Transcript kept in the French Institute of Pondicherry T. No. 592.

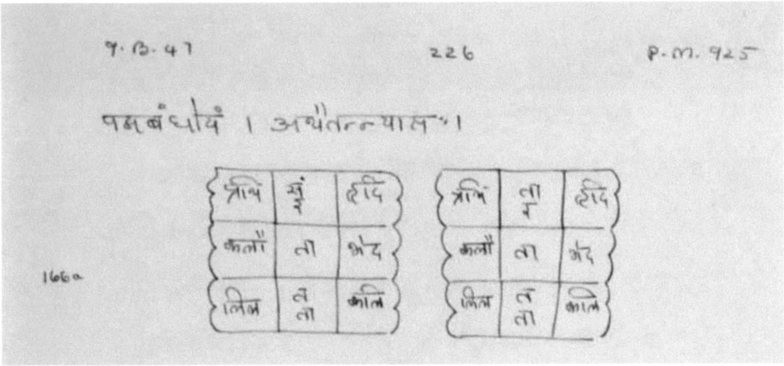

The category *gati*, described next by Bhoja, comprises palindromes and related figures that involve more than one way to read, or complicated ways to read, as in the "horse" (*turaṅga*) reading, derived from the movement of the horse in chess.

The key principle of most of these image poems lies in the intricate way of reading and repeating syllables, as for instance, in the complicated *gomūtrika*, where one can read the same verse either in a normal way or zig-zag between lines.[1] But what we need to bear in mind before we look at European samples is that all Indian varieties described by the poeticians are in fact centred on the single verse—and thereby limited in size—, and project a certain way of reading onto an image, which need not stand in connection to the content. The image is mainly a visual representation of the reading technique, drawing the image is not part of the artistic endeavour. This is left to the scribes and their modern incarnations, the editors.

We now return to the idea of an Indian primacy in *citrakāvya* quoted above from Jha's article. Even Ernst's excellent book cannot escape the Indian *Zeitgeist*, for there too we find the notion that the Indian visual poem, which supposedly reaches back before Christian times, could have instigated occidental visual poetry.[2] The idea could go back to Kalānāth Jhā's treatment of the Vedic antecedents of *citrakāvya*, as for instance the so-called "riddle hymns" of the Ṛgveda.[3] But the confusion arises simply because the term *citrakāvya* is much wider than "visual"

[1] The term literally translates "cow urine" and is supposed to be derived from the zig-zag pattern formed by the urine of a walking cow. [2] "Die Überlegung, das indische Figurengedicht, das vielleicht bis in die Zeit vor Christi Geburt zurückreicht, könne die abendländische visuelle Poesie mitangeregt haben, erscheint kühn, aber nicht absurd." Ernst, *Carmen figuratum: Geschichte des Figurengedichts von den antiken Ursprüngen bis zum Ausgang des Mittelalters*, p. 808. [3] Jha, *Figurative poetry in Sanskrit literature*, p. 136.

or "pattern" poetry. According to the Indian taxonomy a riddle (*prahelikā*) can be grouped as *citrakāvya*, but since it has no visual component, it falls by no means into the category of visual poetry.

The background behind the unknown sources of Ernst is nevertheless worth dealing with. Many Indian writers on cultural history follow what is basically a religious article of faith, according to which everything in this world is based on "the Veda". It has to do with colonial history and more recent developments that this religious conviction has become a stock theory in an increasingly nationalistic ambit and with a nationalistic twist. For if everything is based on the Veda, this means that India is the cradle, at least potentially, of all culture, and with a more recent addition, all science. For a long time Indian and non-Indian academics have smiled at these fancy ideas that border on conspiration theories. According to this, the first aircraft, the invention of nuclear physics, genetic engineering or plastic surgery, everything is thought to have an ancient Indian antecedent, usually gained by anachronistic interpretations of Sanskrit texts and by giving fanciful early dates for them. Every Indologist has some training in ignoring this, for instance in the cultural-cum-political speeches given at the beginning of conferences by administrators or politicians, since they do not usually interfere with serious academic work. Recently it has become more difficult to ignore this, because what has before been faded out as a strange folklorist practice not to be taken at face value, has recently transformed into a (pseudo-)academic trend and even an official political program in India.

Fortunately, as far as our present issue is concerned we may cut the argument short, and Ernst himself has identified the main problem:

> "Während die westlichen *carmina figurata* auch in figurierter Form überliefert sind, erscheinen die indischen in den alten Handschriften nur als lineare Texte, die erst von der modernen Literaturwissenschaft aufgrund der Hinweise in den Kommentaren in visueller Form abgebildet werden." [1]

The idea that *citrakāvya* resembles visual poetry in the Western sense is misleading, for it is in fact quite difficult to find specimina of *citrakāvya* that are visual objects in the way a Western reader would expect visual poetry to be. Classical com-

[1] See Ernst, *Carmen figuratum: Geschichte des Figurengedichts von den antiken Ursprüngen bis zum Ausgang des Mittelalters*, p. 808.

mentators may have described how a *bandha* is to be executed, there are schematic drawings in the margin of some manuscripts,[1] and editors have done their best to draw images like *khaḍgas*, *murajas* and the like, but, again, we do not really have corresponding visual objects. To a large extent, *citrakāvya* is still, in full accordance with the ideals of classical Indian poetry, predominantly oral literature.[2]

The rift between the traditions is considerable in this respect. Visual poetry in a variety of European and other languages is ideally transmitted in the physical form of a piece of art, even though in practice early European specimina may not always be available in manuscript form, whereas later specimina were printed right away. Still it is obvious that "visual poetry" can only work, when seen in the intended "visual form". This means that we need to presuppose an audience that reads the text, and not merely listens to its recitation.

On the other hand, many of the techniques in *citrakāvya* can be reconstituted with the requisite technical knowledge. It is sufficient to know that a certain verse is intended to be of a certain type.

Furthermore, to name a *gomūtrika*-verse visual poetry, is a misnomer in so far as the image of "cow urine", which is just denoting a zig-zag line, is not relevant to the content of the stanza nor is it a visualisation of it. There are exceptions,[3] but there is not necessarily and not often a meaningful relation between the image and the content. All this is by no means to belittle *citrakāvya,* which has been neglected for a long time just as many other forms of visual poetry, despite displaying an extreme verbal ingenuity that would deserve much more attention than it has received. It just shows what separates *citrakāvya* from visual poetry, and the reason for emphasizing this distinction here is that it is relevant for a description of the *Kalpavṛkṣa.*

It should also be interesting for Indologists to learn that historians of European visual poetry are quite explicit about important factors in its development, most

---

[1] Some examples are given in Battistini, "Citrakāvya in Manuscripts: the case of Ānandavardhana's Devīśataka." [2] I agree with Vose that the few examples, where such verses are given in the expected "visual" form, the predominance of orality remains unaltered and does not make *citrakāvyas* into visual objects: "While it is intruiguing to see examples of citra verses rendered in pictorial form, I do not believe it detracts from the point that these verse forms also would have been encountered aurally in the goṣṭhī setting." Vose, "Jain Uses of Citrakāvya and Multiple-Language Hymns in Late Medieval India: Situating the Laghukāvya Hymns of Jinaprabhasūri in the 'Assembly of Poets'," p. 324 [3] For instance a string of *citra* verses in a battle scene in the *Haravijaya*, where the images are all military. See Lienhard, "Text-Bild-Modelle der klassischen indischen Dichtung," p. 152.

notably the Byzantine Iconoclastic Controversy[1] and other prohibitions, but also the high profile of Islamic image poetry and calligraphy. This factor, although omnipresent in the Indian cultural landscape, has never been discussed, which well reflects the solipsism of large segments of Indian Sanskritic culture. We should also recount what Ernst states about Jewish visual poetry,[2] namely that the proponents of Jewish studies generally assume an Islamic influence on its development—despite a highly developed emic tradition, and despite the fact that no concrete Islamic sources could be pointed at.

The reason for this brief survey is the following: When we look at the spectrum of Indian *citrakāvya*, it is impossible to fit the *Kalpavṛkṣa* into any of its categories. From the perspective of *citrakāvya* the *Kalpavṛkṣa* is not even impressive. There is no special method involved in reading the text, the base text is just a linear text and the intexts consist of simple lines. There is no repetition of syllables, which is a characteristic of all Indian forms. But also seen from the perspective of how the *Kalpavṛkṣa* works, there is not much that tallies with the characteristics of the *citrakāvya* genre. The *Kalpavṛkṣa*, as we have seen, consists of clearly defined elements: (1) One continuous large (Śāstra-)text in prose and verse forms the basis of a cross-word layout. (2) The intexts are in multiple languages. (3) The intexts form the (aerial roots of a) wish-fulfilling tree, an image that can be related to the content of the work. None of these elements can be fitted into known categories of *citrakāvya*, the first and main point of divergence being that the principle of base text and intexts does not occur in any other known Indian specimen.

The more one reviews *citrakāvya*s, the more one notices the incongruities. As Lienhard makes clear, in *citrakāvya* the relationship between the syllables of the poem and the image are often rather loose, and thus *ākāracitra*s would fall under shape poetry ("Umrißgedicht" oder "Ausfüllgedicht").[3] Quite obviously the *Kalpavṛkṣa* is something else.

[1] See Ernst, *Carmen figuratum: Geschichte des Figurengedichts von den antiken Ursprüngen bis zum Ausgang des Mittelalters*, p. 756. [2] See Ernst, *Carmen figuratum: Geschichte des Figurengedichts von den antiken Ursprüngen bis zum Ausgang des Mittelalters*, p. 773. [3] See Lienhard, "Text-Bild-Modelle der klassischen indischen Dichtung," p. 153, who also points out that the examples 11 and 12 in the appendix to Jha's monograph, a flag and a club, have the same text.

The *Kalpavṛkṣa* as a *carmen cancellatum*

Descriptions of European visual or pattern poetry are no less complex than the Indian ones. All philologies tend to have their own specific perspectives and discourses, and categories are not always laid out in the same manner. In the following I shall mainly follow the highly sophisticated system of Ulrich Ernst[1], which, though focussed on European medieval specimina, is fairly comprehensive and comparative—it even contains a chapter on *citrakāvya* with relevant insights also for Indologists. The terminology used is partly German, partly Latin, and I shall give an overview here, for this background is necessary for conceptualizing what the *Kalpavṛkṣa* is, and what it is not.

The Latin term *carmen figuratum, Figurengedicht,* or "figure-poetry", denotes a combination of text and image, in which the text[2] is written to resemble a figure that stands in a meaningful relation to the content of the text. The European medieval specimina are usually religious, and thus religious images, often simple Christian crosses, abound. This distinction is important, since text filled into a shape ("figurale Schriftflächen"), an ornamental technique that also occurs in medieval manuscripts, constitutes a separate type. There is also the related term *Umrißgedicht,* "shape poetry", where the distribution of lines and possibly selection of metrical structures allow the text to be written into a specific shape.

The category that bears most resemblance with the *Kalpavṛkṣa* is the "Gittergedicht" or "lattice poem", where text is filled into a kind of chessboard with one syllable per square. The square does not constitute the image, but the figura is created through "intexts" (*versus intexti*), which are marked by colour, as in our text, or, in some specimina are written in majuscule. Typically, in this category the intexts are not always representing a discernible image, since the resulting straight lines cannot form more than geometrical patterns. Since many European specimina are religious and the shape of the intext is quite often a Christian cross, this distinction has often no practical consequences. In view of this limitation, Ernst states that the geometrical type remains on the outskirts of the *carmen figuratum*. The *Kalpavṛkṣa,* as we have seen, would be an exception, for if compared with a

[1] Ernst, *Carmen figuratum: Geschichte des Figurengedichts von den antiken Ursprüngen bis zum Ausgang des Mittelalters.* [2] In Western perspective this text is usually "metrical" poetry. Ernst includes "lyrical texts in the widest sense" (p. 7) and for Sanskrit literature it is natural to include prose *kāvya* as well as mixed genres between *kāvya* and *śāstra.*

"Gittergedicht" of a normal length of 30 by 30 squares, its structure with 150 by 150 squares is more flexible and allows more elaborate and varied intext shapes.

A further distinction is determined by the question whether patterns created by the intexts are just lines that produce outline images, or fill larger shapes with colour, thus creating a more vivid image. These cases are termed *imago*-Gedicht.

One other categorisation depends on the intexts. Do they function merely as visual embellishment ("ausschließlich visueller Textornat" [1]), which Ernst explains as something that cannot be heard in recitation, but is merely seen in manuscript. An example would be an acrostic, to which the reader is alerted by a visual marking of the syllables concerned, but which may easily be lost on the hearer.

Here we can add an Indian specimen of an acrostic as a counter-example, where the acrostic is strangely the main text. Ratnakaṇṭha's *Sūryarahasya* "Secret of the Sun-god" [2] is a brief poem, where the cryptic reference to a "secret" in the text is supposed to lead the reader to the insight that the whole text is an acrostic: the first syllables of each stanza taken together form the Gāyatrī-Mantra. With this verse the text has an unexpected social dimension, for according to classical and conservative Hindu law this Vedic prayer can only be recited by the three upper classes of society. However, the technique to insert the prayer syllable by syllable into a longer litany is a circumvention of these rules and enables, as the author implies, lower casts to use the prayer. But apart from this, Ernst's opinion that acrostics, mesostics etc. do not alone constitute figurative poetry makes sense.

The *Kalpavṛkṣa*, if we want to categorise it in modern European terms, is quite obviously a *carmen cancellatum.* [3] The term was used already by Optatianus Porfyrius, who in a collection of such poems, written around 342 A.D., called them *carmina cancellata.* [4] What is crucial here is that the basic principle behind Sāhib Kaula's *Kalpavṛkṣa* is found only in European *carmina cancellata*, but nowhere in Sanskrit literature.

---

[1] See Ernst, *Carmen figuratum: Geschichte des Figurengedichts von den antiken Ursprüngen bis zum Ausgang des Mittelalters*, p. 539. [2] See Ratnakaṇṭha, *Ratnakaṇṭhas Stotras: Sūryastutirahasya, Ratnaśataka und Śambhukṛpāmanoharastava*, p. 23. [3] "In der Technik des *carmen cancellatum*, in einen Buchstabenteppich eine Figur einzuwirken, der wiederum *versus intexti* einbeschrieben sind, ahmt Hraban den Optatianus Porfyrius und seinen Lehrer Alkuin nach [...]". Ernst, *Carmen figuratum: Geschichte des Figurengedichts von den antiken Ursprüngen bis zum Ausgang des Mittelalters*, p. 225. [4] Carmina 22,2. Quoted from Rühl, "Panegyrik im Quadrat: Optatian und die intermedialen Tendenzen des spätantiken Herrscherbildes."

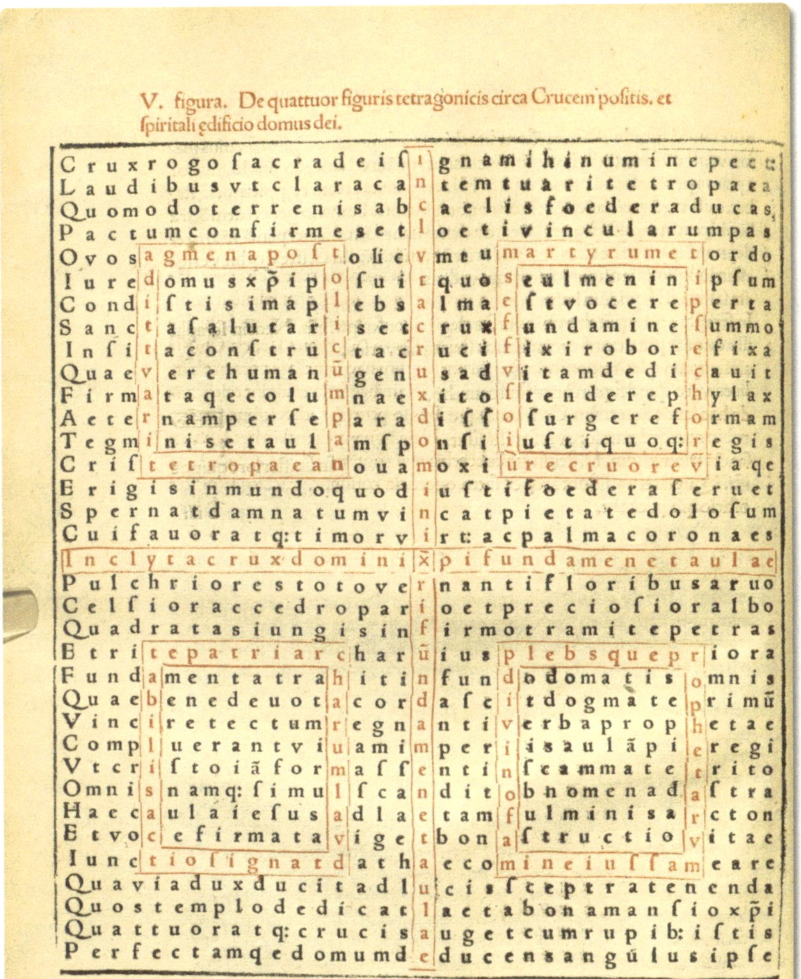

HRABANUS MAURUS: De Laudibus Sanctae Crucis. Digitale Sammlung der Universitätsbibliothek Frankfurt, Ms. lat. qu. 59.

The only insecurity in giving this identification lies in the fact that while Sāhib Kaula might have tried first to follow the idea behind this type by placing one *akṣara* per square, he must have abandoned the idea in the course of composition. The *Kalpavṛkṣa* is therefore something between a *carmen cancellatum* (with one syllable per square) and a form, where the text in between intexts is not determined by squares and therefore not of fixed length. Since the author was using a cloth with squares and started with the first method, he obviously had a concept resembling a *carmen cancellatum* in mind. But if we look at the right side of the cloth, where two red intexts are leading downwards in a straight line, we could also characterise it as a lattice poem with mesostics, for—as we have seen above—no fixed amount of text is found between the two red lines and to the right of the last intext. Since similar failures of authors to stick to the strict principles are known, I would describe the *Kalpavṛkṣa* as a *carmen cancellatum.*

The *Kalpavṛkṣa* shares one other trait with its European counterparts: the intexts are not just there to produce an image, but their contents stand in various intertexual relations with the image, but also with the base text. [1]

Sāhib Kaula leaves it to the imagination of the reader to interpret the title. But I think that the following connection can be made: the red lines on the cloth are intended to represent a wish-fulfilling tree imagined as a Banyan tree with its areal roots. It is wish-fulfilling in the sense that it yields to the onlooker a large variety of poetical and philosophical texts as well as a maximum of languages.

What is less obvious is the link between form and content. I would argue that the author has consciously tried to connect the image, the intexts, and the content of the main text in an abstract philosophical framework: we may understand the wish-fulfilling tree as the tree resembling the supreme reality (*brahman*), which is manifesting in language sounds (*śabda*). The reader would get this idea from the beginning of the base text, which revolves around the question of *śabdabrahman* and its levels. Usually these sounds are those of the Sanskrit language, but here the intexts suggest that we may add a considerable variety of other languages as well.

If we compare the Indian and the European specimina of visual poetry, we may wonder about possible influences. It should have become clear that Sāhib

[1] See Ernst, *Carmen figuratum: Geschichte des Figurengedichts von den antiken Ursprüngen bis zum Ausgang des Mittelalters*, p. 715: "Die *versus intexti* figurieren nicht nur für den linearen Text, sie introduzieren und interpretieren ihn auch, mit einem Wort: sie schaffen ein komplexes intratextuelles Beziehungsgeflecht."

Kaula's piece of art has not much resemblance to Indian *citrakāvya*, but a considerable one to medieval European visual poetry. Only there do we find the basic principle missing entirely from the Indian literary scene: a large image formed by intexts hidden within a primary, base text, as in the types of lattice poem or *carmen cancellatum*.

With the present state of knowledge we cannot say whether Sāhib Kaula had seen other traditions of visual poetry, whether occidental or middle-eastern, but what we can say is that the specific technique used by him does not point to a conclusive inner-Indian development. It also remains to be seen whether or how many similar objects become known, or whether the *Kalpavṛkṣa* stands completely on its own. Admittedly there is no positive argument to prove that Sāhib Kaula has seen European samples, but let me just remind the reader that two centuries earlier Albrecht Dürer's etching "Dudelsackpfeiffer" was reproduced on an ivory box in Sri Lanka not too long after its publication. [1] I see no reason why an author who goes to such a length and visualise the multitude of languages by even incorporating an Arabic quotation would not take the opportunity to adopt a new technique for producing visual poetry. There are quite a few European works printed before the time of Sāhib Kaula, which contain descriptions, theories, or poetical justifications for producing the much-maligned visual poetry. Around the time of the production of the *Kalpavṛkṣa* the Carmelite monk Paschasius published a *Poesis artificiosa* (1674), which contains a description of the *carmen artificale*—to be distinguished from the *carmen naturale*—which is not only of poetic value, but especially valued in religious contexts. Here our intercultural strands unknowingly connect. [2]

But this observation of parallelism is neither proof of an influence, nor it is an explanation of Sāhib Kaula's work. The genre is marked by an extreme creativity and even if Sāhib Kaula's concept behind the *Kalpavṛkṣa* might have some intercultural ramifications, his execution in detail is not only one of a kind, but also one of superlatives not shared by any other known specimen. The sheer size of the base text of the *carmen cancellatum*, with its 45 folios of ornamental prose including 230 stanzas, is probably unequalled in world literature, as is the use of roughly thirty different languages for the intexts. The admittedly ambitious interpretation of the

[1] See Jordan Gschwend and Beltz, *Elfenbeine aus Ceylon: Luxusgüter für Katharina von Habsburg (1507 - 1578)*. [2] See Ernst, *Visuelle Poesie: historische Dokumentation theoretischer Zeugnisse. Band 1: Von der Antike bis zum Barock*, p. 934.

geometrical figures as the aerial roots of this wish-fulfilling tree, which evokes the image of a Banyan tree, yields another layer connecting the image and the text. Furthermore the multitude of relations between the base text, the intexts and the image are no less impressive, even if this "tree" does not grant such wishes as their interpretation too easily, as the present study shows.

Conclusion: The Hidden Context

If we did not have the author's remark about the intended recipient of the cloth, we would be completely in the dark about the context of Sāhib Kaula's *Kalpavṛkṣa*. This issue surrounds many pre-modern Sanskrit works and in some cases it is probably wise to abstain from speculating too much and infer backgrounds that might turn out to be highly imaginative. The context of the production of *citrakāvya* may be such a case. European scholars of Indian poetry as a rule were not too fond of these types of poetry, and here the agreement of ancient Indian critics with European sensibilities was reassuring: "None of the authors, except perhaps the Agni Purāṇa, goes as far as calling this thing poetry, but several treat of it because of its obvious function of entertaining the same audience [...]".[1] But this is hardly an explanation of the phenomenon, which because of its sophistication can hardly be called just a popular pastime.

Perhaps the fact that it was not just written for the same audience, but also by the same authors of "true" poetry[2] should make us rethink the matter. Fortunately we are not completely in the dark about likely contexts for the production of this "artistic" poetry. In a recent article Steven M. Vose[3] has described how the Jain monk Jinaprabhasūri composed and recited poetry in an assembly at the Delhi court of Sultān Muhammad bīn Tughluq in 1328 to impress the sovereign. Whether intended or not, the encounter had rather concrete effects on religious politics: one statue of Mahāvīra that had been seized from a temple was returned, and a number of royal edicts were passed that improved the situation of the Jain community. Vose suggests that his performance at the royal assembly might be reflected in the three artistic hymns that we know of this author, one containing

[1] Gerow, *A glossary of Indian figures of speech*, p. 176. [2] We can ignore here the European notion that by the time *citrakāvya* was written, Sanskrit poetry had already moved into its decadent, artificial, manieristic—many terms have been used—phase. [3] For the following see Vose, "Jain Uses of Citrakāvya and Multiple-Language Hymns in Late Medieval India: Situating the Laghukāvya Hymns of Jinaprabhasūri in the 'Assembly of Poets'."

citra forms, the two other being multiple-language hymns. In both cases, the aim seems to have been to impress the audience with a display of poetic virtuosity. The *Kalpavṛkṣa* might have done well in such a context. Moreover, it does not presuppose a sophisticated training, which would be needed to understand the finer points of the construction of the *bandhas*, and it would include speakers of a variety of languages. Surely it was written for maximum effect.

Perhaps the "dazzling" (*citra*) effect of this literature was not primarily aiming at poetic peers. The critics were probably not the *sahṛdayas* of the *dhvani* school that one likes to think of. True, they might have acknowledged the technical mastery, but could have easily sneered at the lack of true poetic invention (*pratibhā*). The *citra* "performance" might have rather aimed at sponsors and politicians, at a courtly audience of half-experts that could be impressed in public recitations and competitions. For those who have been puzzled by the fact that this artistic form of poetry has been and remained popular despite its low status in literary theory, this is a valuable explanation.[1]

Here it is fascinating to compare European contexts. Despite the clear rejection of visual poetry as "monsters in the literal sense",[2] we find that sometimes the context of their production was as political as that of Jinaprabhasūri. For instance, the collection of *carmina cancellata* by Optatian was written in exile, and the highly artistic panegyric had a very concrete aim, namely to appease Constantine, and possibly revoke the sentence of exile. Apparently the method worked, since one chronicler mentions for the year 329 that Optatian was freed from exile when he sent the text to Constantine.[3]

Then there is one Gittergedicht written by an Italian teacher at a religious school, Eugenius Vulgarius, in the early tenth century. This poem, too, was not written for purely artistic reasons. Eugenius had defended some religious practices of Pope Formosus in writing, but when the pope was condemned and even his corpse mutilated, his erstwhile defender Eugenius was incarcerated. It seems

[1] "While several scholars have taken a descriptive approach to citrakāvya, they have not regarded the context of its performance as a key to understanding its longevity." Vose, "Jain Uses of Citrakāvya and Multiple-Language Hymns in Late Medieval India: Situating the Laghukāvya Hymns of Jinaprabhasūri in the 'Assembly of Poets'," p. 314. [2] LEVITAN, W., "Dancing at the End of the rope. Optatian Porfyry and the Field of Roman Verse", In: *Transactions and proceedings of the American Philological Association* 115 (1985), p. 246. Quoted from Rühl, "Panegyrik im Quadrat: Optatian und die intermedialen Tendenzen des spätantiken Herrscherbildes," p. 75. [3] See Rühl, "Panegyrik im Quadrat: Optatian und die intermedialen Tendenzen des spätantiken Herrscherbildes," p. 75.

that it was in detention that he wrote a number of metrically ambitious poems of praise in order to appease the new pope. It is among these writings that the Gittergedicht was found.[1]

So let us return to the introductory passage,[2] which contains the important historical reference to *Yaśovat Siṃha* (Jaswant Singh).

The circumstances under which Sāhib Kaula was entreated by the ruler to write this composition—if this is to be taken at face value—are unknown. There might have been different aims, political or other, but the only thing we know is that while the recipient may not have been an ingenious warlord, he was a "vernacular intellectual", an accomplished writer and part of a movement, in which works on Advaita Vedānta were composed in Brajbhāṣā. Williams summarizes his pertinent works as follows:[3]

> Jaswant Singh (r. 1638–78), the Rathore king of Marwar (located at Jodhpur), composed several works of religious scholarship in Brajbhasha, all of them styled as dialogues: the Ānandavilās (1667), in which the metaphysical system (tattvajñāna) of Advaita Vedanta is presented in the form of a dialogue between the eighth-century Shankaracharya and an anonymous 'jīv' (being); the Anubhav Prakāś (n.d.), a similar work in which questions of metaphysics and ontology are explored in the form of a dialogue between guru and disciple; the Aparokṣasiddhānt (n.d.) begins with an extended praise of God (guṇgān), but transitions into a discussion of spiritual practice (sādhanā) as a means to attaining liberation; the Siddhāntabodh (n.d.), on the other hand, though also a discussion of Advaita puts notable emphasis on the importance of anugraha or the grace bestowed by God or the Guru onto the spiritual seeker; and the Siddhāntasār, a discussion of tattvajñān that gives extended attention to the futility of pursuing worldly desires. Jaswant Singh also composed 'translations' of Sanskrit texts, including the Gītā Māhātmya (n.d.), a translation and

[1] See Ernst, *Carmen figuratum: Geschichte des Figurengedichts von den antiken Ursprüngen bis zum Ausgang des Mittelalters*, p. 372f. [2] See above, p. 15. By the way the historical reference contained in the work is lost in the Muktabodha transcript, where we read *mahārājayamevat siṃhābhidhāna*, whereas in the manuscript we actually find *mahārājayaśovatsiṃhābhidhāna*. [3] See Williams, "Sacred sounds and sacred books: A history of writing in Hindi," p. 217ff.

> commentary on the Bhagavad Gītā, and—following in the footsteps of Keshavdas— a translation of the Prabodhacandrodaya (n.d.).

Thus both authors might have had common literary interests, as for instance, the idea to fuse the religious and the literary sphere. But nothing is known as yet beyond this point. The presenting of the *Kalpavṛkṣa* might have been a gift by a religious leader and poet to a ruler with congenial literary interests, a meeting of like minds. However, any exposure to the actual facts of Kashmirian history should make the reader aware that this could turn out easily as a romantic projection. Take the turbulent life of the Kashmirian poet Bilhaṇa, who had to leave Kashmir because of problems with the king. The fanciful accounts of his imprisonment and the composition of the *Caurapañcāśikā* when facing execution need not be taken at face value, but Kalhaṇa in his *Rājataraṅginī* (7.935–37) mentions his exile from Kashmir and his reception as court poet at the court of the king of Karṇāṭa as a historical fact.

But here, at the end, we ought to repeat that the *Kalpavṛkṣa* is not even a *citrakāvya*. It does not seem to have Indian antecedents, and we do not know whether the striking parallels to European *carmina cancellata* are accidental or presuppose a direct influence. What we do know is that if entered into a competition, it would probably be the largest piece of visual poetry ever written and the one with the most languages in its intexts.

Manuscript Hs. or. 12509

"Indische Sammelhandschrift" – A brief overview

The Staatsbibliothek Berlin has given this name to Hs. or. 12509 from the Janert Collection, which contains on its 1321 pages a fairly large number of partly fragmentary texts. In the catalogue by Ehlers a few of the texts are identified,[1] but it is worth describing this manuscript in more detail, as I hope will become clear in this chapter. Since the ms. is available as a scan, the pages of this pdf-document (1–1321) are given as reference, for this is presumably the form, in which the reader will access the codex. There is also a pencil pagination (1–557) as common in Western libraries, to which I will refer occasionally, as well as multiple Śāradā paginations of individual texts, which will not be mentioned.

This Śāradā codex belongs to a class of comparatively small oblong leather bound booklets with a considerable number of pages, a format that is known from Kashmir for collections of small texts or anthologies.[2] In our case one major section of the manuscript is transmitting texts of Sāhib Kaula and his disciples, including even one text by his teacher Jñānānāndasvāmin.[3] What is peculiar is the fact that this booklet was intentionally designed for collecting small text fragments in additional (originally) empty pages. The manuscript in its original state consisted

[1] See Ehlers, *Indische Handschriften. Teil 19: Die Śāradā-Handschriften der Sammlung Janert der Staatsbibliothek zu Berlin - Preußischer Kulturbesitz.* [2] For a more elaborate description of this format, sometimes called *guṭaka*, see now Formigatti, "Guṭakas between Book Cultures. The Voelter Manuscripts in the Tübingen Library." [3] Sāhib Kaula's teacher is mentioned as Jñānasvāmin in a colophon. Since the *Svānubhavollāsa* has rather distinct parallels to Sāhib Kaula's *Citsphārasārādvaya* and the fact that this text is transmitted in our manuscript and in a further manuscript within texts of other Kaulas has led to the conclusion that this Jñānānandasvāmin is in fact Jñānasvāmin, Sāhib Kaula's teacher. For an edition and more details, see Hanneder, *Sahib Kaula's Works.*

of a number of texts, already in a few hands that were bound together, but with a considerable number of empty leaves inserted between individual texts. These folios were apparently used by readers to add more texts, or memorable quotations, or stanzas attributed to famous authors. Some of these readers are even known: On page 573 there are three colophons mentioning three successive generations. It seems that owners and readers have turned this manuscript into a small anthology and the way the manuscript was produced suggests that this was more deliberate than the usual Kashmirian practice of using the additional "flyleaves" between texts.[1] In the following we shall describe some details of this interesting manuscript, before the text relevant for the *Kalpavṛkṣa* is edited.

As an example, here is the first folio with transcription:

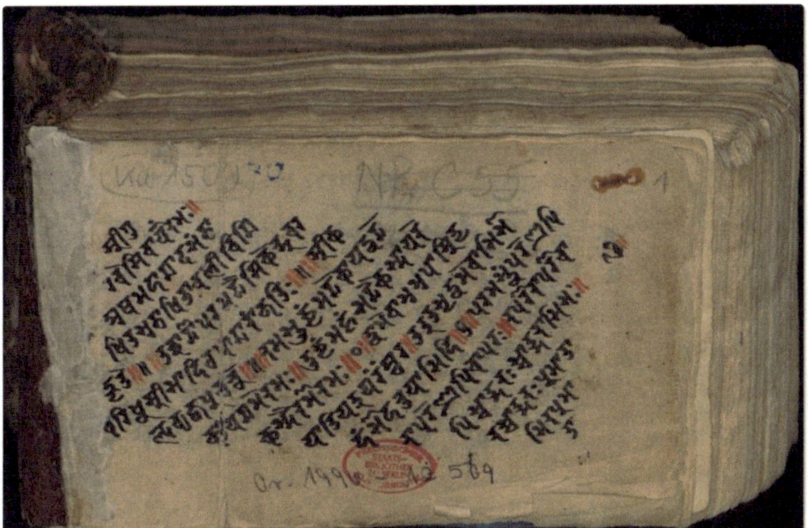

śrīgurave śivāyoṃ namaḥ || atha mahācāryasaṃbhāṣitasubhāṣitāvalī vicittry(?)-ate || tatrādau paramadaiśikendravaravariṣṭhaśrīsāhibapādānāṃ kṛtiḥ || śrīkalpa-vṛkṣaprabandhe ||

[1] "Er füllte nach Kaschmirischem Gebrauch die "flyleaves" der von diversen Händen abgeschriebenen Stücke [...] mit kleineren Stotras, etc., um das im 17. Jahrhundert offenbar noch theuere Papier nicht unbenützt zu lassen." M.A. Stein, in a letter to Johannes Hertel. Dated 14.9.1904. University Library Leipzig. NL 271/1/22/19. I am very grateful to Anett Krause for providing me with this quotation.

namas tubhyaṃ madekāya tvadekāya ca me namaḥ ||
tubhyaṃ mahyaṃ sadaikasmāy anekasmai namo namaḥ ||1||

tvām evāmum upāśritya yāti yatra ya īśvaraḥ ||
tatra tasya tvam evāsi so 'haṃ so'hantayāsi hi ||2||

paramas tvaṃ pareṇāpi nāpareṇāpi vā paraḥ ||
na paro nāparo vāpi svātmanaḥ svātmanāsi saḥ ||3||

na svātmanaḥ pramātāsi na pramātā [...]

The text is a selection of verses from the metrical part of the *Kalpavṛkṣa*, namely verses 1,6, 18 and 26. On the next folio (4) the diagonal text ends, and we find further unrelated notes: brief quotations from the *Mṛtyujidbhaṭṭāraka*, the *Trikahṛdaya*, and the *Vijñānabhairava*.

On such additional pages a change of the direction of writing usually indicates the start of another text fragment. This technique is frequently and creatively employed in this manuscript, as an example from the end of the text shows:

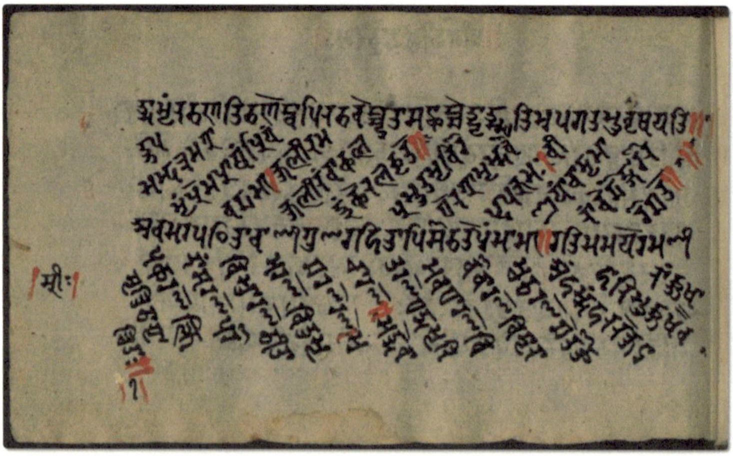

Elsewhere in the manuscript, additions are added to the bottom or margin of a page and written diagonally, but in this text, called *saṃkīrṇapaddhatiḥ* (1196ff),

this technique of writing in various directions is used in a more systematic and creative way. However, the principle remains the same: texts are written in different directions in order to indicate that they do not belong together.

Coming back to the beginning of the codex, the next folio contains three quotations from different texts, all set apart by various directions of writing. Folios 3^{r}(6) and 3^{v}(7) are empty, folio 4^{v}(8) again has two brief quotations, from the *Vijñānabhairava* and the *Tantrāloka*. It is only then, on 4^{r}(9), that a longer text begins. This, presumably, was the text with which the manuscript originally started. In other words, the first four leaves of this codex were empty before binding. The additional leaves might have been added for protection—as a half-title and an additional page in European printing, which are also used for notes—, but since this practice is not very common in Indian mss., I would regard this manuscript as a working exemplar for scholars, comparable to an interleaved copy of a book as it has been ordered from the bookbinder by European scholars. Throughout the manuscript at least two additional folios were added between texts,[1] whereas at the end of the codex we find more additions, so that one can assume that the book ended with a higher number of empty pages.[2]

The codex can be described as an anthology centering on the Kaula clan and its literary output, but it contains also other texts that were widely known in Kashmirian monist Śaivism. Most texts are in Sanskrit, others are in Kashmiri or are multilingual. We find, for instance, the autobiography of Sāhib Kaula, written in Kashmiri, as well as the vernacular *Yogavāsiṣṭhasāra* by Kavīndrācārya Sarasvatī.

If we count all fragments and named authors of fragments, the number is beyond one hundred. This previously undocumented, highly individual method of producing anthologies is an interesting phenomenon, but only cataloguers and textual critics in search for manuscript sources are likely to encounter them. And for the latter their practical value is limited, since the textcritical status of the text fragments is problematic. Are they testimonia, which implies second rate sources for an edition, or should they be reckoned as "normal" manuscripts? All depends on how we think that they were written. Are they notes copied from another manuscript? Are they from a complete text or again from a medley of quotations?

[1] This becomes clear from sections where the empty pages were only partially used. On p. 72 ends a quotation from the *Tantrāloka* with a colophon, on p. 73 we have four brief fragments written as usual in different directions. Then follow four empty pages before the next text. [2]

Or was it simply a verse heard quoted by others that was later written down from memory? It is impossible to decide.

We may note, although this will hardly come as a surprise, that the fragments are never properly identified. Only a name of the author or of the text is given, sometimes nothing is known at all and a verse is marked solely by *kasyāpi* "by someone", i.e. "author unknown".

A large section of the main texts (ignoring the additions) is devoted to works by Sāhib Kaula and his successors. Many additional verses by the same group of authors, sometimes arranged into small collections can be found on the added folios between the main texts. Here is a list of the complete and larger texts from this group:

2	Sāhib Kaula: *Kalpavṛkṣa*
37	Sāhib Kaula: *Devīnāmavilāsa*
39–55	Jñānānandasvāmin: *Svānubhavollāsa*
55–62	Sāhib Kaula: *Śivaśaktivilāsa*
62–66	Sāhib Kaula: *Śivajīvadaśaka*
95–121	Sāhib Kaula: *Citsphārasārādvaya*
122–142	Sāhib Kaula: *Sahajārcanaṣaṣṭikā*
143	Sāhib Kaula: *śrīsāhibakaulapādānāṃ kaśmīrabhāṣayā kṛtiḥ*
171–183	Sāhib Kaula: *Svātmabodha*
191–246	Sāhib Kaula: *Saccidānandakandalī* (with Bhāṣā version)
274–280	Sadānandakaula: *Sadānandalāsya*
284–290	Jyotiṣprakāśa Kaula: *Gurustotra*
399–424	Sāhib Kaula: *iti śrīmacchrīmahāmāheśvarācāryavaryaśrīsāhiba-kaulānandanāthaviracitā bodhamālā nānādeśabhāṣārūpiṇī*
439–444	Sāhib Kaula: *Śārikāstotra*
465–476	Sāhib Kaula: *atha kalpavṛkṣaprabandhāntarvartiniśśeṣadeśa-vibhāṣā vicitryate*
503–519	Govindakaula: *Gurustutiratnāvalī*
569	Sāhib Kaula: [...]*śrīsvāmisāhibapādānāṃ kṛtiḥ*
640–644	Govindakaula: *Svacchandamaheśvarāṣṭaka*
833–905	Sāhib Kaula: *Janmacarita*
1309	Sāhib Kaula
1313	Sāhib Kaula: *svāmisāhibapādānāṃ*

1314	Sadānandakaula
1315f	Cidrūpakaula
1319	Govindakaulasya
1320f	Sadānandakaula

There are clearly many scribal hands involved in the whole codex and obviously the additions are written in hands differing from the hands of the main texts. While there is more than one hand at work in the main texts, I am not always very confident that the very similar hands can be objectively distinguished or identified. Nevertheless, the bulk of the "Kaula" related works was written by one person. In these texts rubricated *daṇḍa*s are systematically used, which together with an orderly style of writing gives these texts a certain uniformity. Quite a few of them are dated by the same method (no other texts in the codex are dated). If we disregard all pages with additions that are inserted between the "main" texts, then the first segment, where all texts are written clearly by the same hand—ignoring of course the added leaves between texts—is formed by pages 15–393.

Within this segment there are a few highly interesting colophons. The first on folio 61f (page 121) gives the name of the author, of the scribe, and a date:

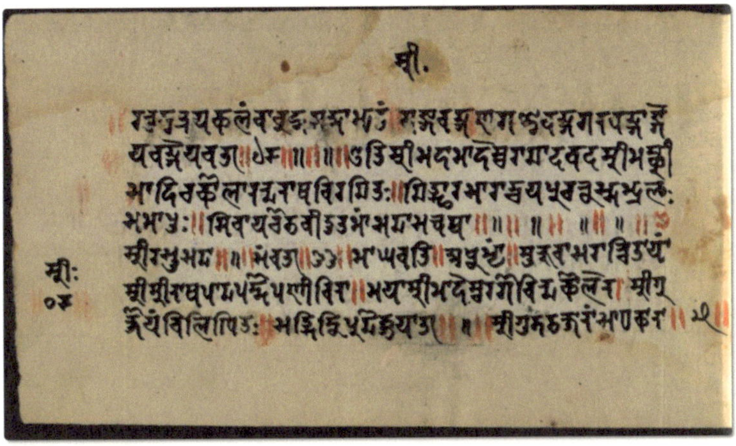

[…] *iti śrīmahāmāheśvarācāryavaryaśrīmacchrīsāhibakaulānanda-nāthaviracitaḥ* || *citsphārasārādvayaprabandhas sampūrṇaḥ samāptaḥ*

|| *śivāya bobhavītutamāṃ sadā sarvathā* || *śrīr astu sadā* || *saṃvat* || 33 || *māgha vati* || *aṣṭamyāṃ* || *śukravāsarānvitāyāṃ śrīśrīnāthapādapadmopajīvinā* || *mayā śrīmāheśvaragovindakaulena śrīgrantho (')yaṃ vilikhitaḥ* || [...]

As can be seen in the image, the layout is orderly, *daṇḍa*s are used systematically and are rubricated. The scribe was Govinda Kaula, who calls himself in other colophons a disciple of Jyotiṣprakāśa Kaula, who in turn was a disciple of Sāhib Kaula.

In the other texts up to page 482, there are clearly other hands involved, whereas on 503–519 we encounter Govinda Kaula as scribe, but here of his own *Gurustutiratnāvalī*. This is one of the very few indubitable cases of a pre-modern Sanskrit autograph, as the colophon on p. 518f shows:

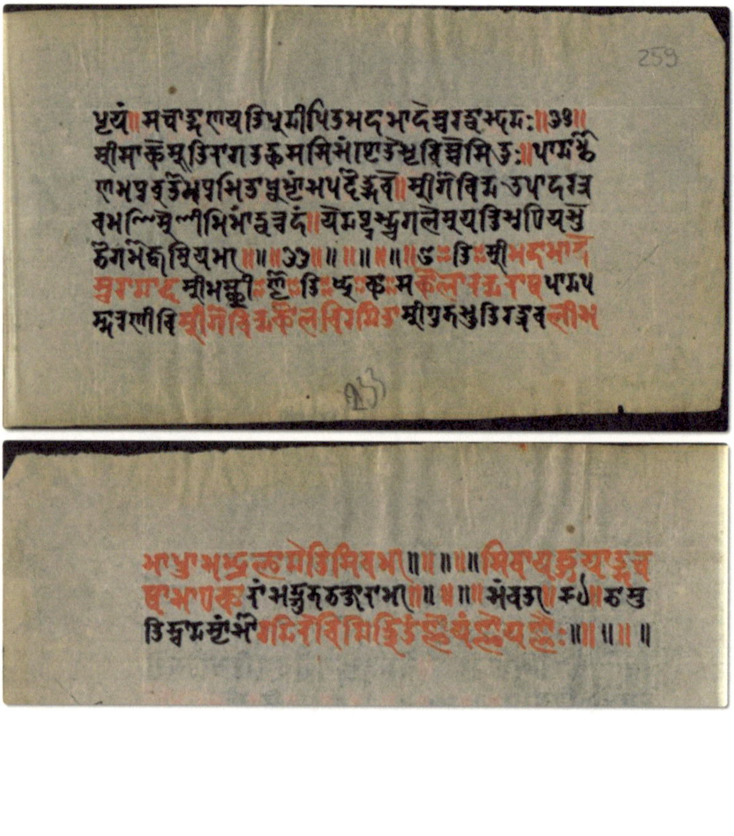

iti śrīmahāmāheśvarācāryaśrīmacchrījyotiṣprakāśakaulānandanātha-pādapadmānujīviśrīgovindakaulaviracitā śrīgurustutiratnāvalī samāptā sampūrṇā ceti śivam śivāya bhūyāt sarvathā sādhakānāṃ sad-gurubhaktānām saṃvat 46 bhā śuti dvādaśyāṃ sauradine vicitritaṃ jñeyaṃ jñeyajñaiḥ

While the names in the colophons are quite clear, the dates provided by Govinda Kaula most probably fall into the middle of the 18th century.[1]

A tentative history of this codex would be as follows: The nucleus was written by Govinda Kaula, who was collecting in it works of his own teacher and other famous authors of the Kaula clan. To this were added other texts written partly by himself, or by others, which means that the codex could have been considerably smaller, or not yet bound, when in Govinda's possession.[2] He also added a text of his own to the collection. With this the Kaula related texts contained in this codex become high-level sources, for they represent the version in the personal copy of a main successor of the author(s).

We would assume that this historically valuable manuscript passed through the generations of the Kaula family, and we do find three names in the "notebook" pages of what were probably later owners, or readers, where authors of brief quotations seem to identify themselves:

[1] For a detailed discussion of the evidence, see Stainton, *Govinda Kaula: Evidence for His Dating, Lineage, and Literary Activity*. [2] It is interesting to note the scribe's remark before giving the colophon to the *Kāmakalāvilāsa*: He says that he had to stop with an incomplete text here, because no manuscript for the rest was available (*ataḥ param ādarśābhāvān na likhitam*).

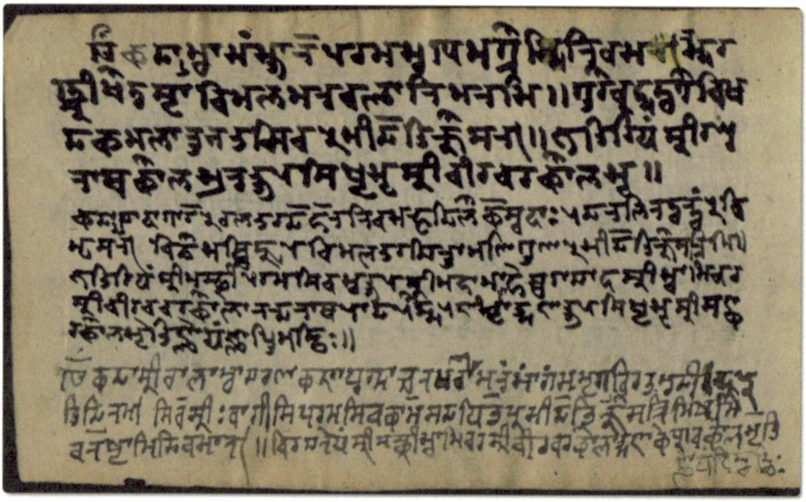

The upper third of the page is a quotation with a concluding colophon: *kṛtir iyaṃ raghunāthakaulasūnurūpaśiṣyasya śrīvīravarakaulasya*, so the quotation is by one Vīravara Kaula, who was son and disciple of Raghunātha Kaula.

To this, Śaṅkara Kaula, son and disciple of Vīravara seems to have added another text and a colophon, although with a typo[1] and correction: [...] *śrīvīravarakaulānandanāthapādapadmopajīvyātmajarūpaśiṣyasya śrīmac-chaṅkarakaulasya* [...] There we find a minute interlinear correction *vyā* in *-jīvyātma-* for *syā*.

The last third of the page contains a third quotation by a third hand in faded ink with the colophon: *viracaneyaṃ śrīmacchrīsvāmivaraśrīvīravarakaulātma-jakeśavakaulasya* [...] Here another son of Vīravara with the name of Keśava seems to have added a text and identification. Some of these may have been later owners of this codex.

For reference here is a more comprehensive, but still incomplete list of texts and fragments in Hs. or. 12509:

[1] The manuscript actually reads *vīravavara*.

2–3	Sāhib Kaula: *Kalpavṛkṣa* (see above)
4	*Mṛtyujidbhaṭṭāraka, Trikahṛdaya*
5	*Sarvajñānottara, Tantrasadbhāva*
8	*Vijñānabhairava, Tantrāloka*
12	*Bhargaśikhā*
16–22	*Devīrahasye mahāgaṇapatikavaca*
23- 36	Abhinavagupta: *Parātrīśikāvivṛti*
37	Sāhib Kaula: *Devīnāmavilāsa*
39–55	Jñānānandasvāmin: *Svānubhavollāsa*
55–62	Sāhib Kaula: *Śivaśaktivilāsa*
62–66	Sāhib Kaula: *Śivajīvadaśaka*
67–72	*Tantrāloka*
73	*Mahānvayaprakāśa (sic), Cidgaganacandrikā, Pañcastavī, Ambāstava*
78–85	Śaṅkara: *Kaivalyopaniṣaddīpikā*
85–90	*Bhṛṅgīśasaṃhitāyāṃ Cidīśvarastotra*
95–121	Sāhib Kaula: *Cidsphārasārādvaya*
122–142	Sāhib Kaula: *Sahajārcanaṣaṣṭikā*
143	Sāhib Kaula: *śrīsāhibakaulapādānāṃ kaśmīrabhāṣayā kṛtir*
144–164	*Lallāyoginīvākyāni*
165–167	*śikhnordīnasya* [= Sheikh Nur-ud-Din?]
171–183	Sāhib Kaula: *Svātmabodha*
191–246	Sāhib Kaula: *Saccidānandakandalī* (with Bhāṣā version)
249–250	unidentified fragments
251- 254	Ratnakaṇṭha: *Ratnoddharaṇāṣṭaka*
254–258	10 verses (*kasyāpi*)
259	*nīlasya, śaraṇasya*
260	*umāpatidharasya, kasyāpi*
262	*kasyāpi*
264	*mahākaviśrīmayūrasya*
266	three verses from Ratnakaṇṭha: *Ratnaśataka*
267	twice *kasyāpi*
268	2 verses from Ratnakaṇṭha: *Ratnaśataka*
269	*kasyāpi*
270–273	*tantrasadbhāve piṇḍabrahmāṇḍavyāptiḥ*

274–280	Sadānandakaula: *Sadānandalāsyastotra*
281–283	various quotations from Abhinavagupta, *Saṃvidullāsa*
284–290	Jyotiṣprakāśa Kaula: *Gurustotra*
291–393	*Kāmakalāvilāsa*
399–424	Sāhib Kaula: *Bodhamālā nānādeśabhāṣārūpiṇī*
426–429	Cidrūpakaula (disciple of Sāhib Kaula): *Gurubhaktistotra*
429–30	Akabharīkālidāsasya goṇḍamiśranāmnaḥ padyatrayam
434–35	Gauḍīrāgiṇī, Khaṭarāgiṇī
439–444	Sāhib Kaula: *Śārikāstotra*
444–448	*Skandapurāṇe* devīgāthādaśakaṃ
449–453	*Śukāṣṭakam*
453–456	*Gaurīdaśaka*
457	*Tantrasāre*
458	*atha dhāraṇamantraḥ* (and further fragments)
459–460	unidentified (non-Sanskrit)
462–464	(new hand, non-Sanskrit)
465–476	(Sāhib Kaula:) atha kalpavṛkṣaprabandhāntarvartiniśśeṣadeśa-vibhāṣā vicitryate
476	fragment attributed to Madhusūdanasarasvatī
477–478	unidentified fragments
482–500	*atha kavikāvyapraśaṃsā* various authors: *kasyāpi, śrībāṇa-bhaṭṭamahākaveḥ, govardhanācāryasya, vallabhadevasya, jal-haṇasya, trivikramabhaṭṭasya, jagaddharasya, ratnakaṇṭhasya* etc.
503–519	Govindakaula: *Gurustutiratnāvalī*
523	*atha caturdigguṇavarṇanam*
524	*atha raṇastutiḥ*
535	*mahākavimayūrasya*
538	*akabharīkālidāsasya*
543	*kālidāsasya*
548	*bālajībhaṭṭasya*
550	*jalhaṇasya*
552	*raviguptasya* (end of the collection)
553	unidentified fragment
557–558	fragments, *rājānakaratnakaṇṭhasya, tasyāpi*

546–565	*gītagovinde pañcamaḥ sargaḥ*
569	*atha samasyāpaddhatiḥ*, then fragments in different hands
573	Vīravara, Raghunātha, Śaṅkara and Keśava Kaula (see above)
575–586	Rāmakṛṣṇakavi: *Bhagavatīpadyapuṣpāñjali*
588–598	*atha sajjanapaddhatiḥ* (different authors)
600–603	*atha khilāḥ*
609–619	*vyāsamuninā viracitaṃ śivanirvāṇastotram*
620–623	*Bhavānīstuti*
624–639	Maheśvarānanda: *Parimala*
640–644	Govindakaula: *Svacchandamaheśvarāṣṭaka*
647	*atha śivastavapaddhatiḥ* collection from different sources, end more and more fragmentary
686	*athānyadevastutiḥ*
693–710	*atha śrīśivabhaktiḥ rājānakaratnakaṇṭhakṛtā*. Page 710: *kṛtis tasyaiva*
713	*etāni sarvāṇi vṛttāni rājānakaratnakaṇṭhasya*
714–717	from the *Stutikusumāñjali*
721–764	Śaṅkara: *Tripurasundarīmānasikopacārastotra*
769–783	Kṣemarāja: *Parāpraveśikā*
789–813	*Sāmbapañcāśikā*
815	*atha prabodhapaddhatiḥ* [...] Madhusūdanasarasvatī
816	*vṛttayugmaṃ māheśvarayogānandasya*
817–822	*Mokṣopāyeṣu*, *Kulārṇavasya*, Śivasvāmin, etc.
827–831	*Mokṣopāya*
833–905	Sāhib Kaula: *Janmacarita*
908	unidentified fragment
909–972	Maheśvarācārya: *Kaśmīrabhāṣāṇi padāni*
975–987	various fragments
991–1010	various fragments
1013–1126	Kavindrācārya Sarasvatī: *Bhāṣā-Vāsiṣṭhasāra*
1127	verse of Sudarśanakaula
1134ff	various fragments, (1196) *atha saṅkīrṇapaddhatiḥ*, (1243) *praśnottararatnamālikā*
1245–1307	*iti śrīdaśāvatāracaritacitritā khaṇḍapraśastiḥ*
1309–1321	various fragments

From here onwards almost all pages have additions written in other directions. We find a non-Sanskritic quotation from Sāhib Kaula (1163), a *saṃkīrṇapaddhatiḥ* (1197ff), a *praśnottararatnamālikā* (colophon on 1243) and as the last longer text one part from the *Daśāvatāracarita*.

The last folios are again devoted to quotations from the Kaulas and here it seems Govinda Kaula has already become a historical author from whom verses are collected as of the other Kauls.

1309	Sāhib Kaula
1313	Sāhib Kaula
1314	Sadānandakaula
1315f	Cidrūpakaula
1319	Govindakaula
1320f	Sadānandakaula

While this codex shows very clearly how a study of the details of manuscripts can assist prosopographical studies, it is by historical accident that this important document surfaced in a collection in Berlin, within easy reach of the present writer. Without the notice of this manuscript by Ehlers in his catalogue, it could have taken quite long to unearth its value. Therefore, to conclude, I quote a verse from one of the poetical anthologies in our manuscript:

ye tāvan malayopakaṇṭhanilayas teṣv indhanaṃ candanaṃ
tīropāntanivāsināṃ jalanidhe ratnāni pāṣāṇavat
kaśmīrāntaravāsinām api nṛṇāṃ nātyādaraḥ kuṅkume
dūrasthasya mahārghatā paribhavaḥ saṃvāsato jāyate

For those whose home is near the Malaya, Sandal is just firewood.
For those who live on the shore, pearls in the ocean are just stones.
People living in Kashmir have no great regard for saffron.
What is invaluable from a distance is disregarded by those living near.

With this we shall return to Sāhib Kaula's *Kalpavṛkṣa*, more specifically to the text on pages 465–476, which has no real title, but a descriptive colophon stating that it contains all the vernacular quotations in the *Kalpavṛkṣa*.

Facsimile Edition

One obstacle in identifying the non-Sanskritic intexts woven into the *Kalpavṛkṣa* lies in the Kashmirian spelling of foreign languages in Śāradā script. Here the cloth written in Nāgarī was of some help. Often Kashmiri scribes write modern vernaculars in Śāradā script just as they would transcribe other foreign languages. Due to the Kashmirian pronunciation of the *javarga*, non-Kashmiri and non-Sanskrit words with *ja* are transcribed in Śāradā in a kind of diacritical mode as *jya*. In Śāradā no distinction between *śya* and *cya* is visible, which means that both may stand as diacritical transliterations for *śa* or *ca*. Furthermore, aspirated consonants are not sufficiently distinguished in Kashmirian pronunciation from non-aspirates, which does not usually affect Sanskrit orthography, but that of other languages, as visible even in the variant spelling of the authors name as either *sāhiba* or *sāhibha*. Taken together this means that the word जब may be represented as *jyabha* in Śāradā script. One also needs to bear in mind that there is a frequent confusion between *ī* and *e*, which are pronounced the same, and occasional confusion of aspirated and unaspirated consonants, and there is sometimes no distinction of Śāradā *ḍā* from *ḍa*.

Below I shall give a facsimile of the Berlin manuscript with diplomatic transcription and added variants from one or more cloth versions where possible. Quite often the cloth and Ms. version are identical. Where possible the left row adds the location on the cloth in the format [line.row].

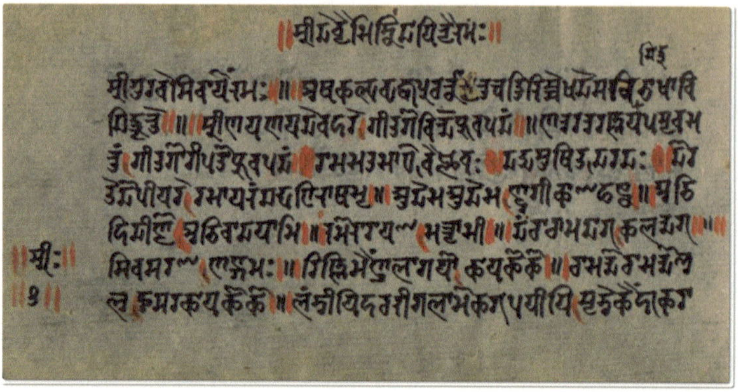

atha kalpavṛkṣaprabandhāntarvartiniḥśeṣadeśavicitrabhāṣā vicitryante:[1]

[1]	śrī jaya jaya deva hare || *gītagovinde dhruvapadaṃ*
[115.11]	janur anurañjaya[3] paśya vasantaṃ || *gītagaurīpatau dhruvapadaṃ*
[111.26]	rāmasatasādho, vaiṣṇavaḥ
[131.38]	datṛśuṣita daradaḥ (C_3 dardaśuthita)
[117.19]	doratedopīyare
[-]	rasāyanaṃ carpaṭināthasya
[110.16]	ādesa ādesa || jyugī kānahaṭṭa
[109.7]	(a) abhihidījyo ||
	(b) abhivādayāmi ||
[102.22]	namo nārāyaṇa | sannyāsī ||
[130.9]	daṃbābāmadār ||
[-]	kalandar ||
[105.?]	śiva śaraṇa
[-]	jaṅgamaḥ
[-]	riñji maiṃ jūlāgayau kāyako ko
[106.?]	bāsando bāsando lulu
[-]	bhuśarakāyako ko
[-]	laṃ ḍīyihabarīgalāmokar payīyi
[-]	cyaḍe kaiṃh karā

[1] The scribe first wrote *prabandhasya*, then deleted the *sya*, and added an *ā*. The author or scribe uses the word *vicitryante* more often in this huge manuscript in places where one expects no more than the sense "write" or "compose".

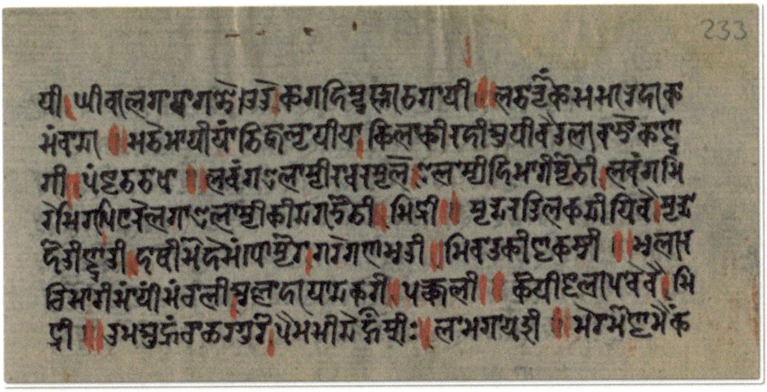

yī

[–] ghīv lagā yā gaṇḍe ote

[–] kāgahicyuñj bhagāyī

[–] labhānyoṃkāsas nuh kā saṃvād

[27.122] sabhe māyīyāṃ bhikṣālyāyīyā || kilā kī nahī āyī vaital vāḍāe kājyugī || *paṃjyābhabhāṣā*
(C3 save māyīyāṃ bhikṣālyāyīyāṃ kilā kī nahī āyī vai)

[–] lavaṃga ilācyīnāvanacyale ilācyī himārī cyobhī

[–] lavaṃgasiresir piṭane lagā ilācyī kī dar ḍobhī || *siṅrī*
(C3 lavaṃga ilācī (?))

[23.130] cyandanatilakadīyi[1] vaicyandā hotī jyutī || hāthī sohesaṃkhācyorā || gare gajamutī
(C3 caṃdanatilakadīyi vaicandā hote jyothīhāthe sohesaṃkhācorāgare jasutīle (?))

[–] mivāta kī jyakaḍī

[–] mul na bisārī sāṃyīṃ saṃbālī

[–] allāh yādakarī || *pakkalī*

[9r.104] ko yī jyāl pāve vai || *siṅrī*
(C3: koyī jālapāve vai)

[1.46] uma āhūṃ bācharaguro paimasīdehuṃ śrīḥ
(C3 uma āhūṃ bāccharguro paimasī)

[–] lāmagāyatrī

[54.40] merāmojya maiṃ ka-

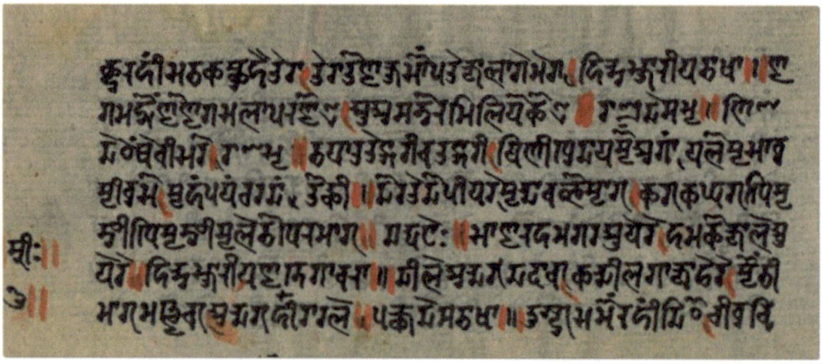

chyu nahīṃ sabhakacchu (kucchu C_3) hai terā || terā to jyakusauṃ pate kyālāge merā || *hindusthānīyabhāṣā*

[–] jyagama hmoṃ jyojyagasalāpanajyoi

[–] ā aśaḍo na miliyo koi || *rāṇūdeśasya*

[–] jiṇade ṭhemthe vīsare || *rāṇasya*

[–] bhayātateṅgarīvataṅgarī

[–] yijī khudāya cyoṃ agāṃ, yalocyasābucyībuso

[–] cyahaṃ payaṃ baradāṃ torkī (totkī?)

[–] dorate dopīyare cyandāvarṇo cyār

[–] kar kappar khicyaḍī khicyaḍī cyale bhokhanamār || *carpaṭeḥ*

[–] sājyanahamagara āyere || hamako kyāle āyere

[–] hindūsthānīyajya ṣāña(?)gāvanā [1]

[36.139] dīle andar daryāv kandīlagā kyā here || cyoṃbhī mār mañjyāv andar hīrārale *pakkadeśabhāṣā*
(C_3: dila andaradarayāvakaṃḍīlagākyāphirecyoṃbhīmārama-jjābu aṃdarahīrārale)

[1.139] tujhyu samoṃ nahīṃ diṭho || bīvuvi
(C_3: tuṃ jhūṃsamo nahidiṭho vī?e)

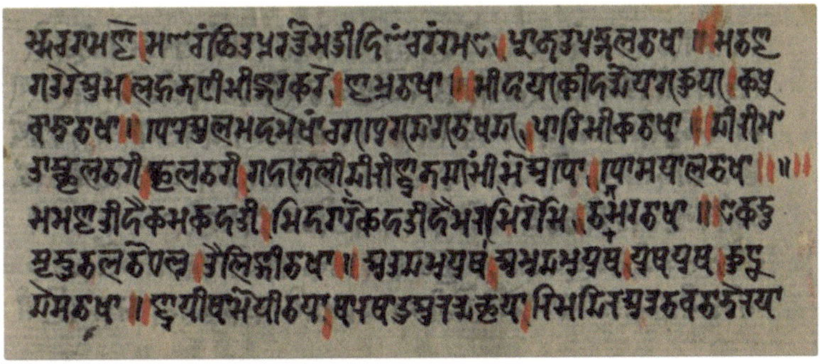

ssabarāmajye || maṇabaṃchitapūranto sattīhiṇaṃ baraṃramai || *prākṛtapudgalabhāṣā*

(C_3: vissambharāmaje maṇabaṃcchitapūranto sattehiṇimbharaṃ ramaī)

[–] sabhajyagatere āsa

[–] lahuruṭīsiṅgārakare || *jyamūbhāṣā*

[–] sīhāy kīhandoyār bhuy || *kaṣṭhavāḍabhāṣā*

[1.90] khāna ālamahameṣāṃbar khur dār bhāṣad || *pārisīkabhāṣā*

[4.109] dīnīmātācchy(ccha C_3)alabharī || cchyalabharī || gah rulī dīnī jyuruc(joruca C_3) sīṃso akhā || *khāśapālabhāṣā*

[7.114] samajyatī hai kamakahatī || miharāroṃ kahatīhaiman sirosi || *bhagasarabhāṣā*

(C_3: samajatī hai kasakahatī miharāro kahatī haimanasirosi)

[–] ikabhucya bhū(?ḍū)bhalabhodhalu || *tailiṅgībhāṣā*

[5.128] atadamuyutha || amudamuyutha || yuthayutha || *bhuḍḍhadeśabhāṣā*

[1.134] jyuyīthāsoyībhayā || thānathātu ānanda chyayā || nisadina anubhavabhāḍenayā

(C_3: joyīthāsoyībhayā thānathātu ānanda cchayā nisadina anubhavabāḍenayā)

(C_2: joyīthāsoyībhayā thānathātu ānanda cchayā anubhavabāḍenayā)

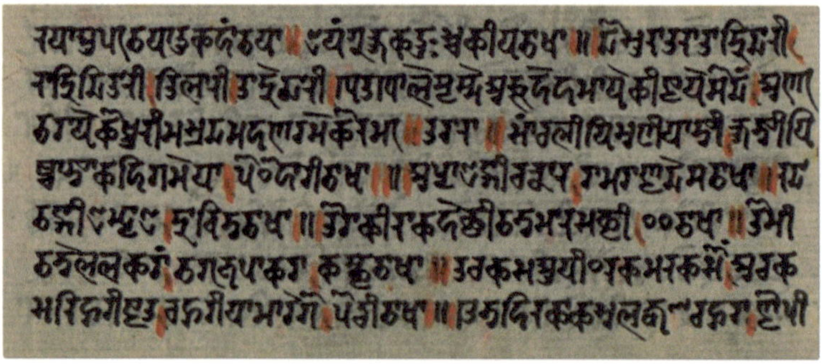

nayā āp bhayātu kahāṃ bhayā || *iyaṃ granthakartuḥ svakīya-bhāṣā*
(C₃/ C₂: nayā āpa bhayātu kahā bhayā)

[1.145] dostanātanātādridānī || nādriditānī || tilānī || tādredānī || khatakhālecyaśme abhruhehamāye kī jyāyemodaṃ || aṇ bharāye koṣṭhunī masūdamahajaramekonam || tarānā || sāṃbalīyimuṭīyāḍī || kuḍīyithvāḍākahigameyā || *poṭhohārī-bhāṣā*
(C_3: dostaṃnātaṃnātādridānī nādredhitāni etc.)

[78.] apyā iṅgībandhāna || *rāmarājyadeśabhāṣā*
(C_3: apyā iṅgevandāna)

[–] nadābhaṅgī ispyāi(?impyāi) || *drāviḍabhāṣā*

[–] torākīnākahechyībhaḍamānasachyī || *ṭhaṭhabhāṣā*

[–] tomībhaḍelalakarāṃ || bhar kṛpākarā || *kacchyabhāṣā*

[–] tabakasa āyīṭhanakamanakasoṃ || abakasanihurījyāta || bahurīyāmārego || *potvībhāṣā*

[18.104] oḍahinakākasulakṣaṇabahurā || jyopī
(C_3: oḍuhinakāgasulakhaṇabhavarā || jyopī)

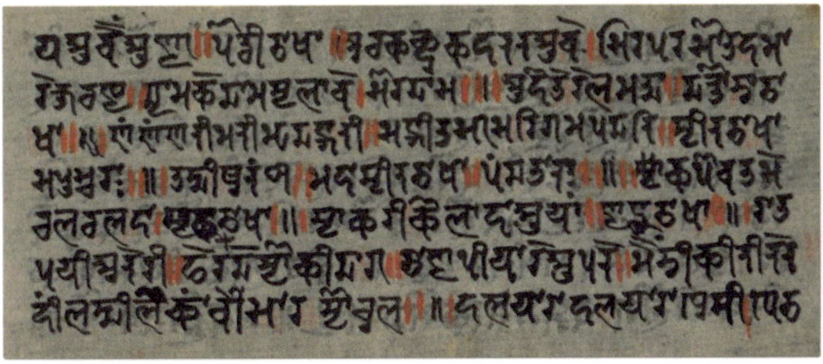

ya āvaiṃ ājy || *poṭvībhāṣā*

[41.136] abakachyukahanana āve || sira para sauta hamāre kubajyā || śyāma ke dāma cyalā ve || *soradāsa*
(C3: ohujī aba kacchukahanana āve sira para sauta sāmāre kubajā || ma ke dāma cālā ve)

[–] āho tere lamardā || *dantauḍabhāṣā*

[104.13r] jaṃjaṃ janī manī mṛdaṅganī || saṅgītam sarigamapadani || *cyīnabhāṣā saptasvarāḥ*
(C3: jaṃjaṃjaṃjanīmanīmirdaṃganī)

[–] uddīthunaṃ (?taddī-) ? || *mahācyīnabhāṣā*
(C3: tadīthunaṃṭhī)

[–] paṃcatānāḥ

[–] kapovatasebalabalahā || *cyakānabhāṣā*
(C3: kapovatasibalabalahā)

[–] cyākarī kolāhā āyāṃ || *jyaṭṭhabhāṣā*

[68.9r] rātapayī anerī || herade cyau kī dar || bhājya pīyāre āpane || maiṃ ḍī kī nīnena hīṃ laddī lokāṃ veīṃ sāra cyaubula ||
(C3: rātapayī anerī phirade cau kī dhāra bāju piyāre āpane maiṃ ḍīkī nīnaladdīlokā vesāra [gap?])

[58.4r] halayārā halayārā khuśī || khabha
(C3: halayārā halayārā khuśe || khabhare)

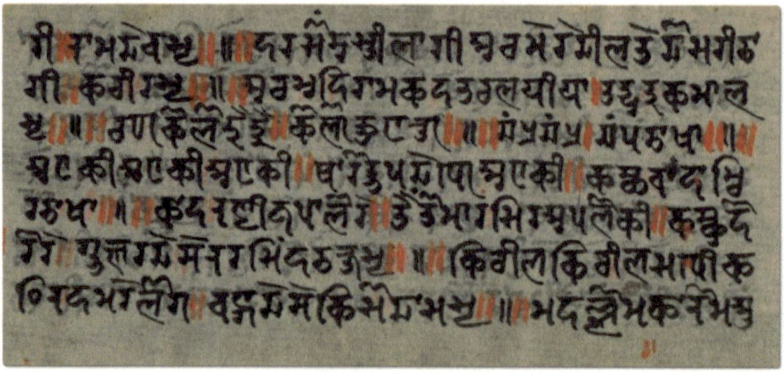

[-]	rī || *nāmadevasya*
[-]	hara soṃ dustī lāgī aba mere dīla te dosarī bhāgī || *kabīrasya*
[94.4]	abamuhi rāma kahata balayīyā || *tatputrakamālasya*
	(C3: abamuhi rāma kahata balayīyā)
[109.3r]	badh kolo draitrai || kolo bhuṭant
[117.3r]	caṃpū caṃpū || *caṃpabhāṣā*
[122.3r]	aṭakī aṭakī aṭakī thārorūpadekh aṭakī || *kacchavāhāmbirabhāṣā*
[-]	kāhana jyī kṛpālo re taiṃ tomāra sira apalokī || kacchu horore || *gurjaradeśe narasiṃhabhaktasya*
	(C3: kāhana jyī kṛpālo re taiṃ tumāra sira apalokī keccu hurore)
[-]	kibīla kibīla sakhī kaṭhina hamare loga || *vaṅgadeśe kisodāsasya*
[74.101]	mahallomakānoma ā
	(C3: mahallobhakāno)

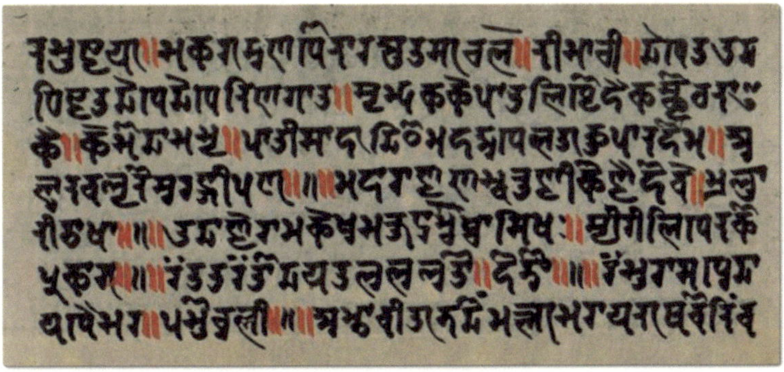

[–] nastajyāy || sakar dujakhonāra ātam bale || nīsāvī

[–] dekhata udadhijyāta dekha dekha nijagāta || cyampakakepāta-likhyo hai kacchyo banāikai || *kesodāsasya*
(C3: dekhata udadhijāda dekha dekha nijagāta || campakakepā-taṅkaccholikhyu hai banāi kai)

[1.23] pātīśāh diṭhomaharmukhalat[1] bhūpā na homa
(C3: pātīśāha diṭhoṃ heramukhalat bupā nūhoma)

[–] arjunavalyano śuraṅgīpaṭ

[1.33] mahārājyajasvantajyī ko jyai hove || *mūluānībhāṣā*
(C3: mahārājajasvaṃtasiṃgha jī kī jeho vo)

[1.122] udājye rāmakeṣu sakuṭumbeṣv āśiṣaḥ || cyīrī likhana ko prakār

[17.9] (a) ī tata ītau dayata lulululutau || hoḍau
(C3: ī tata ītau daitalu luluhatau)
(b) īstarāśa khudāyakhaisara || pastobulī
(C3: īstarāśa khudāyakhisara)

[28.17] ambhāvīt rudoṃ marj (? mall?) sarāyan thavonimva
(C3: ambāvīt rudo maiso mañjasarā yanathāvonimava)

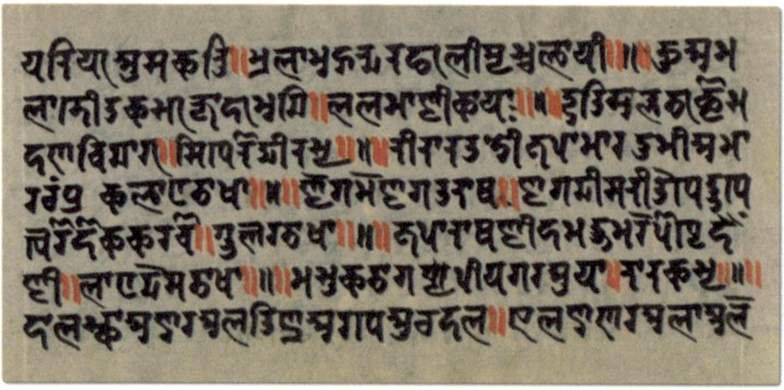

[-] yaniy āśakanti mūlāmuhundanah || līcya svarṇāyī || bhu amalā ñītakas kyāh muci || lalamā jyī kāyāḥ || dyutidurlabh chyo sahaja vicār || *śikhanordīnasya*

(C3: yaniya āśakanti mūlāmuhundanah || līcya svarṇāyī || bhu amalā ñītakas kyāh muci || lalamā jyī kāyāḥ || dyutidurlabh chyo sahaja vicār)

[62.137] nīnānataṇḍī kṛpāsāra(māra?) tumī amārabandhū || *karṇāṭa-bhāṣā*

(C3: nīnāṃnataṃḍe kṛpāmāḍa tumī amāravanhu)

[39.90] jyegame jyagatanātha || jyagadīśanī te khatu(?)kharkha roho ka karavo || *gurjarabhāṣā*

(C3: jegame ja jagadīśane te kharūṃ kharkharo [connection unclear from here.])

[-] kṛpānāthajyī hama bhūmarepokhya haiṃ jyī || *lāṭadeśabhāṣā*

(C3: kṛpānātha jī hamatuhmāre poṣpaheṃ jī)

[88.92] mastakabhāga pīyagara āyā || *nānakasya*

[99.110] hā laskā ajura alatijū arakha ābahal || jālajujara alā ale

(C3: hā laskā ajura alatijū arakha ābahalajālajujara alā ale)

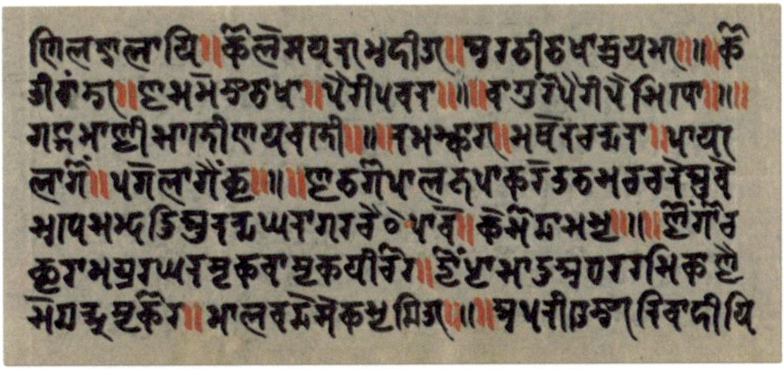

jilajulāyi

[–] koleśayan muhīt || *arabhībhāṣādvayam*

[–] kotīrāṃḍ || *jyasameḍabhāṣā*

[–] pairīpavanā || vāguro pairī paisikhā || gaṅgamājyīsāñī jaya vañī
(C_3: pairīpavanā vāguro pairī paiyasiṣā)

[134.63] namaskār || mathenabandanā || pāy lāgoṃ || pagelā gaiṃ chya

[10.70] jyabha gopāla kṛpā kare tabha saba bane āvesukhasampatti ānandaghanāgaravaiṭhe pāve || *kesodāsasya*
(C_3: jaba gopāla kṛpā kare tabasaḥ babani āve)

[–] jyoṃ gau bachya rāmayūraghanacyakavācyakayībora || dyauṃ pyāsā tu adhararasikā jyaise candracyakora || *mālavadeśe kasyacit*

[38.108] apanī oḍ (?) || nivāhī yi
(C_3: apanītanivāhī yi)

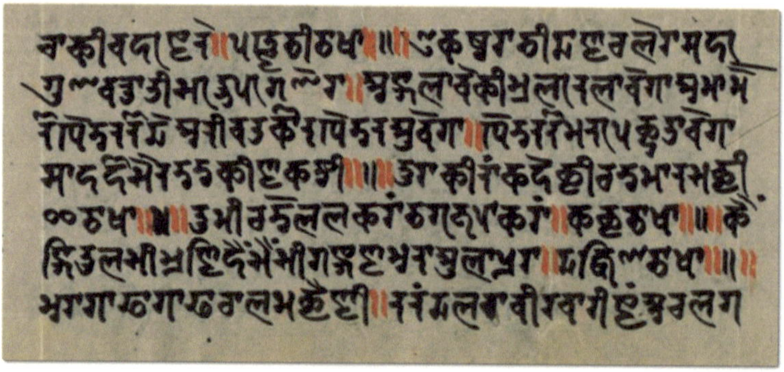

[-] rvā(bā?) kī vah || jyane || *pañjyabhībhāṣā*

[50.128] ikathurābhīdājyabalerāśah guṇavantā tīs rūp gaṇerā || aṅgalāvekī mūl nalāvegā amāmaino kheḍananode anīvata kauna kheḍana āvegā || kheḍana no man pachyutā vegā śāha hosaina ḍaḍa kī jyakaḍī || turā kīnāṃ kahe chyībaḍamāna sachyī || *ṭhaṭhabhāṣā*

(C3: ikathuḍgāvīdājyabalerāśaha guṇavaṃtā tīsarūpaghanerā agalāve mūlanalāvegā amāmaino khiḍanade anīvata kauna khiḍana āvegāvata khiḍanu nomana pacchutā vegā)

[-] tumī baḍelalakarāṃ bhagakṛpākarāṃ || *kachyabhāṣā*

[106.101] kaiṅgi tulasī mūjyi haiṃ saiṃ sī gaṅgājyamunā ālāpūrā || *dakṣiṇabhāṣā*

(C3: kaiṅgi tulasī moji haiṃ saisī gaṅgāyamunā ālāpūrā)

[117.93] murāgāḍhāgāḍhābālamachyaijyī

(C3: murāgāḍā gāḍāvālamachajī)

[107.90] nanaṃda labā vīravārījyāṃ abalaga

(C3: nanaṃda larā vīravārījyā abalaga)

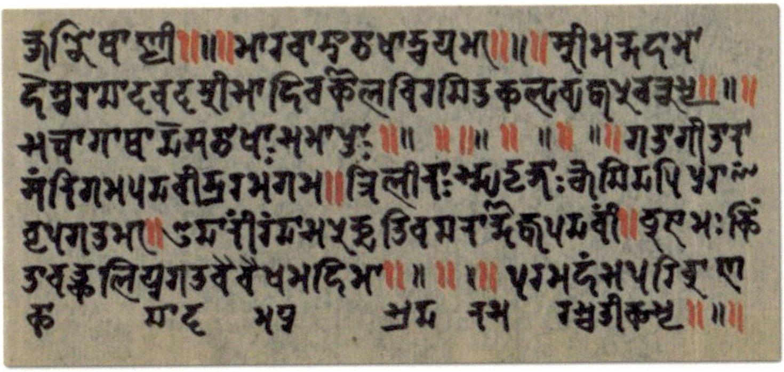

[–] kuṇṭhi(ṇḍi)thājyī || *māravāḍabhāṣādvayam*
C3: kuṇṭhe thājyī

[Colophon:] śrīmanmahāmāheśvarācāryavaryaśrīsāhibakaulaviracitakalpavṛkṣaprabandhasya || sarvā gāthādeśabhāṣāḥ samāptāḥ ||

The Beginning of the *Kalpavṛkṣa* with Auto-commentary

The following sample presents the critical edition of merely the beginning of the *Kalpavṛkṣa* with the commentary of the author. In this part of the text we find an introduction, of which two versions of different length are transmitted, followed by just the first three sentences of the *mūla*-text, but explained in an elaborate *vyākhyā*.[1] This is all there is of Sāhib Kaula's auto-commentary, and the *mūla*-text, on which we have the commentary, is but a tiny fraction of the whole work, corresponding to one folio side out of ninety in the Berlin manuscript (B_4). The commentary is interesting in many respects, and shows that what we might have understood of the complicated *mūla*-text falls painfully short of what the author intended to convey. Here are a few notes.

1. In the beginning of the *mūla*-text (p. 92, l. 1) the word *susvatantra* or *svasvatantra*—*su* and *sva* are homographical in many Śāradā hands—many readers might understand as *svasvatantra*, for this is how the word is edited at least twice in well-known Śaiva works.[2] The doubling of *sva* reminds of another word from the Pratyabhijñā jargon, that is, *svasvarūpa*, and is therefore not suspicious.

Our author disagrees, in the sense that he wants to understand the word as *susvatantra*, which is clear from his gloss *suṣṭhu svatantraḥ* (p. 98, l. 20). The interpretation is confirmed by the editors of the *Devīnāmavilāsa*, who read once *susvatantrā*.[3]

---

[1] This name is given to the text in an additional colophone to $Ś_1$ which runs: *iti kalpavṛkṣavyākhyā/ śrīmatsāhibakaulaviracitā*. But this is most likely just an identificatory term for the text rather than its proper name. [2] *Tantrāloka* 9.53 and *Netratantroddyota* ad 21.31. [3] 7.98, p.142.

2. One of the major techniques employed in the auto-commentary is that of a deliberate proliferation of multiple meanings. The author is obviously fond of complicating the interpretation of key terms by adding a larger number of etymologically based meanings. For example, the term *parākhyā* (p. 101, l. 6) is first (p. 101, l. 14f.) explained as that which has another (*parā*) name (*ākhyā*), but then five further interpretations follow (p. 101, l. 16ff.): as that which expands (*ā-khyā* = *prathanam*) like Śiva (*para*), that which is named as Śiva, etc.

There are more interpretations like this, but the maximum is reached with the word *anuttara,* which is explained in sixteen ways (p. 106, l. 1–p. 107, l. 2), and here the different meanings are even enumerated in the manuscript.

3. In some portions, especially where the commentary is not transmitted by the highly accurate ms. G_2, textcritical problems do remain. For instance, the explanation of *aharārdhagati* (95.3f.)—the word is written without Sandhi and with the initial *a* clearly readable in both manuscripts—should refer to the line *haratu manomalaṃ haraśarīraharārdhagatī* (84.6) in a preceeding verse. The final *ī* stands for *i* in Sandhi, but obviously we cannot read *ahara* in this verse, but we can read (')*harārdhaṃ,* but without *gati,* in another, immediately preceeding quotation (94.13). This looks more like an oversight by the author than a faulty transmission.

4. In another passage I have kept as the name for a source of quotation *vāsiṣṭhe yoge* (97.1), which is the reading in ms. G_2 against the three other mss. that have *vāsiṣṭhe yogaśāstre.* If the author meant to refer to the *Yogavāsiṣṭha,* which is not even clear, this would be the *lectio difficilior.*

There is also an interesting reading in B_4 which adds *ślokasaptakena* to this identification of the text. But while we find quite a few passages containing the required words *tvam aham* in the *Mokṣopāya,*[1] we do not find a sequence of seven verses that would fit.

[1] Often as an enumeration *tvam aham ityādi,* or *tvamahamādikaḥ* sometimes adding *idam,* sometimes referring to *jagat,* etc. (III.1.23c, V.17.34, VI.166.12, VI.193.9, VI.209.39a, VI.256.5a, VI.316.3, VI.322.20, VI.349.31c, VI.363.23), *tvamahaṃśabdakāv api* (3.40.63). *tvamahantādivibhramam* 6.193.10, then *tvamahamādimat* VI.135.2b, *tvamahamādīva* VI.345.70c, and *tvamahamādikaḥ* VI.349.10d.

5. An important philosophical topic the author wants to clarify in the commentary is the relationship between three non-dualistic schools, namely *brahmādvaya*, *śivādvaya* and *mahādvaya*.

Already in the beginning of the shorter commentary, he announces that (92.10ff.) after composing[1] the work itself, he has made "this effort", in form of the commentary, to establish that the three doctrines of *brahmādvaya*, *śivādvaya* and *mahādvaya* are the final doctrine of all doctrines. Since all have non-duality as their ultimate aim, he says that he will feel free to omit hidden meanings, and only deal with the specifics of these three occasionally, implying that these forms of *advaita* are considered by him to be in fundamental agreement.

Then there is a specific reference (96.8–10) to an upcoming passage on these three non-dualist "views", which most probably points to one paragraph in the commentary on the second section (102.21–103.12). There the author first explains the word *vivartamānasya* as *vivartena rajjusarpadṛṣṭāntavat svakalpitamohāvṛtīnāṃ bhāsamānasya* "appearing to those who are veiled by a self-imagined delusion, as in the example of the rope and the snake, through unreal transformation (*vivarta*)". Then he adds that this detail constitutes the distinctive doctrine that separates Vedāntic from Śaiva non-duality: while the adherents of the non-duality of *brahman* adhere to a doctrine of unreal transformation (*vivarta*), the adherents of non-duality of Śiva teach a doctrine of freedom (*svātantrya*), here in the sense that Śiva can veil his nature to produce a universe that seems separate from himself.[2] In Śaiva theology, one of Śiva's powers, called "concealment" (*tirodhāna*), has this function of veiling his true identity. Śiva's freedom consists in his free decision to either veil his nature, which for the individual soul results in transmigration, or to reveal it, which amounts to a liberation of the soul. Here the liberating factor may be knowledge, but it is also by the grace of Śiva, another of his powers, that this knowledge is revealed.

For Sāhib Kaul, in the final analysis, when the specific explanations of how the universe comes about are given up (*vivartam apahāya / svātantryamatim apahāya*), then the one *brahman* or the one *anāśrita*(*-śiva*) remain, which—this is the author's implication—are merely two words for the same non-dual reality. In this way the two schools, Advaita Vedānta and (Pratyabhijñā) Śaivism are brought into harmony, which is one typical trait of author's writings.

---

[1] Lit. "having shown" *vyapadiśya.* [2] *ayam eva ca brahmādvayaśivādvayadṛṣṭyor anyonyaṃ svasvaviśiṣṭhārthaḥ / yad brahmādvayavādibhir vivartavādo nirṇītaḥ śivādvayavādibhiś ca svātantryavādaḥ /*

This type of interpretation, the author adds, should be employed further on in the text: through giving up individual differences between the two philosophies, one shows that they have the same essence of non-dualism.

Here I must mention one rather crucial philosophical difference between the two non-dualisms that Sāhib Kaula does not mention, for it is important for understanding the discussion of one upcoming reading: For the adherents of the Pratyabhijñā school the world is not unreal, but a "real" manifestation of Śiva. When this brand of Śaiva philosophy became popular and was later transmitted in environments that were increasingly dominated by Advaita Vedānta, this doctrine was either not understood, or tacitly ignored—a fact that is even reflected in our manuscripts.[1]

Strangely, the third view (*mahādvaya*) is not explained by Sāhib Kaula, nor is it mentioned elsewhere in his works. But we may find it in the term *parādvaita*, succinctly defined by Abhinavagupta in his *Mālinīślokavārttika*:[2]

> *satyaṃ kiṃtv advaye tattve bhedo 'pi na na yujyate*
> *idaṃ hi tat parādvaitaṃ bhedatyāgagrahau na yat* (1.123)
>
> This is correct, but even duality is not impossible in the non-dual reality. For the supreme non-duality [is not the absence of duality, but] exists, when (*yat*) there is neither rejection nor acceptance of duality.

Abhinavagupta's disciple Kṣemarāja uses the word *parādvaya* in his commentary on the *Netratantra* and there calls it a doctrine that is expressed in all Śāstras only in a veiled manner (*parādvayasya sarvaśāstreṣu gūḍhoktyāsūtritasya* ad 2.11). He mentions different aspects of this notion,[3] and the fact that he refers to an upcoming passage on *parādvayavyāpti* (14.8), but then seems to return to the topic under the name of *mahādvayavyāpti.*[4] suggests that these terms are interchangeable. In his commentary on the *Stavacintāmaṇi* Kṣemarāja also uses both.[5]

This accords well with Sāhib Kaula, who states in another text that *mahādvaya* is the supreme system. Since he quotes Kṣemarāja in the context, we may assume

[1] Ratié has discussed a passage by Abhinavagupta where this problem leads to confusions or even deliberate misunderstandings. Ratié, "Pāramārthika or apāramārthika? On the ontological status of separation according to Abhinavagupta," p. 386. [2] Hanneder, *Abhinavagupta's Philosophy of Revelation. An Edition and Annotated Translation of Mālinīślokavārttika I, 1–399*, p. 78f. [3] *parā- dvayasphurattātmamahāsattārūpaparacaitanyātmani* ad 16.22. [4] *mahādvayavyāptyā sarvatra jīvanmuktiprado* ad 16.24. [5] *mahādvaya* ad 97, *parādvaya* ad 2, and *parādvaita* ad 3.

that the name is reserved for esoteric Kashmirian Śaiva non-dualism. At least this is what the following verse from his *Devīnāmavilāsa* suggests:

> *mahādvaye darśanarājarāje*
> *prasiddhasiddhāpratimaprabhāvaḥ*
> *citiḥ svatantro 'khilasiddhisiddhiḥ*
> *pūrṇo 'pi śūnyo jayasi svabhātaḥ* (3.2)

Here Pāda c refers to Kṣemarāja's *Pratyabhijñāhṛdaya* 1 (*citiḥ svatantrā viśvasiddhihetuḥ*). In other words the term *mahādvaya* refers to one peculiar view within Śaivism, according to which an encompassing non-duality includes duality.

6. One peculiar problem I could not solve lies in variant readings in "Śruti" quotations. In theory quotations from Upaniṣads should not contain problems, since the wording is considered sacrosanct according to its status as *śruti*, and we would expect a Śaiva Vedāntin not to meddle with quotations of his fundamental source texts. But in the real world of manuscripts we do find variants in *śruti* texts[1] and also authors who quote not the established printed text, but something else.

Sāhib Kaul is no exception: he reads *Bṛhadāraṇyakopaniṣad* 4.3.32 as *etasyaivānandasyānyāny ānandāni mātrām upajīvayanti* (98.4), whereas the vulgate has *bhūtāni* for *ānandāni.* His variant reading is shared by all manuscripts and makes good sense in the context. This could be just a scribal corruption, but there is more.

7. A similar case is the quotation that is given merely as *dvaitam eva* (105.10), which refers to *Bṛhadāraṇyakopaniṣad* (Kāṇva) 4.5.15[2]: *yatra hi dvaitam iva bhavati tad itara itaraṃ paśyati*). Here of course a whole philosophy hinges on this *iva*. The context in Sāhib Kaul's commentary is the notion that the subject, be it Śiva or Śakti, cannot be known as an object. For this he quotes the Upaniṣad, according to which a perception of an object is possible in—not in nonduality—, but in duality, literally, where "there seems to be duality".[3]

[1] Hanneder, *To edit or not to edit*, p. 103–127. [2] Corresponding to 2.4.15 in the Mādhyandina recension. [3] Neither Böhtlingk's rendering as "Denn wenn es etwa ein Zweites gibt [...]" (Böhtlingk, *Bṛhadāraṇjakopanishad in der Mādhyaṃdina-Rezension*, p. 30) nor Olivelle's (Olivelle, *The Early Upaniṣads*, p. 131) "duality of some kind" capture the more Śāstric force of the *iva bhavati* as something that only "appears to exist". Compare Slaje: "wo Zweiheit vorzuherrschen scheint" (Slaje, *Upanischaden. Arkanum des Veda*, p. 135).

But one is left wondering whether Sāhib Kaula did not in fact mean *dvaitam eva*. We have seen above that the *mahādvaya* doctrine encompasses duality and non-duality, and so the knowledge of reality does not simply obliterate duality, it rather includes it in a higher non-duality. If Sāhib Kaula was trying to infuse this idea into the quotation, he might well have read *yatra hi dvaitam eva bhavati* "where there is only duality". From this *mahādvaya* perspective, liberation is a state that does not exclude duality, whereas the state of the bound soul should be one, in which "only duality" prevails. Again, there is no way to prove whether this was an intentional twist by the author, or a simple misreading in the archetype.

8. It is with the commentary on the third section starting with *tata eva* that a first topic takes shape. The author says that the preceeding passage was meant to summarize the nature of *parā vāk* and that he will now turn to *paśyantī*, so the topic is obviously the levels of speech according to Bhartṛhari: *evaṃ tāvat parāsvarūpaṃ saṃgṛhya paśyantīm āviṣkaroti tata eveti.* The author then quotes three verses on the three levels of speech from Bhartṛhari's *Vākyapadīya*, but with variants, which in view of the insecurity of even famous quotations, I have not corrected.

The Apparatus

In the edition the first apparatus lists all variant readings, the second apparatus adds testimonia and further information.[1]

The format of the apparatus is simple: the accepted text stands left of the bracket, the variants are right of the bracket. Each entry is followed by the siglum of the manuscript. The entry

7 *tat* coni.] *tatra* B_4 om. $Ś_2$

would mean that in line 7 the reading of the critical text is *tat*, which is based on a conjecture, while B_4 reads *tatra*, and $Ś_2$ omits the word.

Corrections are given by specifying the reading before correction (ante correctionem) and after correction (post correctionem). The entry

tat $Ś_1^{pc}$] *ta* $Ś_1^{ac}$

indicates that ms. $Ś_1$ has corrected *ta* to *tat*.

[1] For a list of manuscript sources and sigla, see p. 7.

कल्पवृक्षः

[mūla text, first section]

श्रीमच्छ्रीसुस्वतन्त्रानाश्रितनिर्भागपरमप्रकाशविमर्शमयपारमैश्वर्यानुभावानुभावुकप्रथितमहितनिजसहजपरमानन्दाद्वयसत्तासामान्यस्पन्द उदितोदितपरमशक्तिसाम्राज्यो राजराजेश्वरो जयसि परमशिवस्त्वमयम् ॥

[The briefer introduction according to Ś$_2$ and G_2]

स्वातन्त्र्यतन्त्रं स्वात्मान्तर्भावैकनिपुणं परम् ।
परस्थं स्वपरात्मानं संस्तुमस्तं महेश्वरम् ॥

निजकल्पवृक्षबन्धे तीर्थ्यानुग्राह्यनोदनावशितैः ।
साहिबकौलपदस्थैर्विरच्यते स्वल्पतात्पर्यम् ॥

इह खलु मरुवाटदेशविशेषाधिपतिमहाराजयशोवत्सिंहाभिधानप्रार्थनावशीकृतहृदयेन कश्मीरदेशवरलब्धाविर्भावसाहिबकौलाभिधस्वारामकृतस्थितिना केनचन कल्पवृक्षबन्धं व्यपदिश्य ब्रह्माद्वयशिवाद्वयमहाद्वयदृष्टीनां सर्वतन्त्रसिद्धान्ततां प्रतिपादयितुं श्रमोऽयं स्वल्पो बालबोधनार्थं व्यधायि । अत एव गूढार्थसंस्कृतिपरिहानम् । तत्र तासां तिसृणां महादृष्टीनां अद्वैतप्रतिपादनमेव परमार्थः । किन्तु कुत्रापि कुत्रापि स्वस्वदर्शनार्थविशेषोऽपि प्रतिपादितः । तद्विशेषविरोधपरिहारार्थमेवास्य यत्तस्य कृतकृत्यता ॥

[The longer introduction according to Ś$_1$ and B_4]

इह खलु मरुवाटदेशविशेषाधिपतिश्रीमन्महाराजयशोवत्सिंहाभिधानप्रार्थनावशीकृतहृदयेन श्रीमत्कश्मीरदेशवरलब्धाविर्भावश्रीमच्छ्रीसमग्रकौलकुलशिरोमणिस्वच्छतरसमस्तषड्दर्श-

2 In the mūla text some words are illegible because of a broken margin in G_2: च्छ्रीस्वस्वतन्त्रा, र्यानुभावा 3 त्वमयम् B_3Ś$_2$] त्वमय G_2 4 स्वातन्त्र्यतन्त्रं G_2] स्वातन्त्र्यं Ś$_2$ 11 संस्कृति G_2] संस्कृतपद Ś$_2$ 14 विशेष Ś$_1$] विशेषविशेष B_4 14 प्रार्थना B_4] प्रार्थनया Ś$_1$ 15 कौलकुल B_4] कौल Ś$_1$

नसिद्धान्तसाराग्रगण्यमहान्तःकरणेन श्रीमत्साहिबकौलाभिधस्वारामकृतस्थितिना केनचन केनापि चिद्विलासेन ब्रह्माद्वयशिवाद्वयमहाद्वयदृष्टीनामद्वैततताप्रतिपादनपुरःसरां सर्वतन्त्रसिद्धान्ततां प्रतिपादयितुं अस्य श्रीकल्पवृक्षाभिधप्रबन्धस्य गद्यपद्यादिवाक्यरचनारचितस्य शाखाफलपुष्पादिरचनारचितस्येव साक्षात्कल्पतरोः प्राक्प्ररोहं समुल्लिखितवता तथा चाहमाध्वनिकस्तत्कुलजातिमान् बालानामिव स्वल्पबुद्धीनां तद्विचारनिःश्रेणिसमारोहणाशक्तानां गूढार्थसंस्कृतपदपरिस्फोटनाय तत्तद्विशेषविरोधपरिहानाय च निजकारुण्यदृष्ट्या तत्स्वल्पतात्पर्यरचनाविधौ कटाक्षितः सन्यथामति व्याकरोमीति तत्र तावद्ग्रन्थादौ विघ्नध्वंसनपूर्वकसमाप्तिकामः स्वेष्टदेवतानमस्कारलक्षणं मङ्गलं विदध्यान्मनसि विहितमपि सद्दृष्ट्यपाठकानुशासनाय गद्यपद्यक्रमेण छन्दसोपनिबध्नीयाच्चेति शिष्टिराचारश्चेत्येतन्मतमाश्रित्य ग्रन्थकृत्स्वपद्यं विवृणोति स्वेष्टेशीति ॥

स्वेष्टेशीनतितनुमङ्गलं स्वचित्ते
निर्णीयाभिलषितपूर्णतावसानम् ।
धीराणामनुगणनाय शास्त्रवक्त्रे
कुर्वेऽहं स्वरचितपद्ययुग्मकेन ॥

स्वस्य स्वेषां वा इष्टा स्वेष्टा सा चासावेशी स्वेष्टेशी । तद्विषयिका तत्कर्मका वा या नतिस्तत्तनुस्तत्स्वरूपं यन्मङ्गलं तत्स्वचित्ते स्वकीयमनसि पूर्वं निर्णीतमपि सच्छास्त्रवक्त्रे कर्तुमारब्धे ग्रन्थादौ कुर्वे उपनिबध्नामीत्यर्थः । ननु प्रयोजनासद्भावान्मङ्गलकरणे प्रवृत्तिः साहसिकीत्यत आह अभिलषितपूर्णतावसानमिति इतो मनोवाक्कायकर्मभिरभिलषितस्य इष्टस्य ग्रन्थस्य या पूर्णता पूर्तिः विघ्नविध्वंसपूर्विका समाप्तिः तत्रावसानमतो यस्य अवसानं फलं यस्य वा इत्यर्थः । मङ्गलस्य समाप्तिः फलं विघ्नविध्वंसस्तु अवान्तरो व्यापारः इति प्रपञ्चः । नवीनास्तु मङ्गलस्य विघ्नविध्वंस एव फलं समाप्तिस्तु बुद्धिप्रतिभादिकारणकलापादिति अस्माकं तु प्रौढमङ्गलकरणशक्तानां तादृग्बुद्धिप्रतिभादिरहितानामुभावेवेष्टाविति । अथ च मन एव मनुष्याणां कारणं बन्धमोक्षयोरिति अभियुक्तोक्तत्वात्पूर्वं मनसि निर्णीतं

---

5 जातिमान् $Ś_1$] जनिमान् B_4 6 कारुण्यदृष्ट्या $Ś_1$] कारुणदृश्या B_4 9 सद्दृष्ट्य $Ś_1$] सदृष्य B_4 9 गद्यपद्यक्रमेण $Ś_1$] गद्यपद्यत्रयेण B_4 15 इष्टा B_4] इष्ट $Ś_1$ 15 काय $Ś_1$] कावा B_4 18 इतो $Ś_1$] इत्तो B_4 20 समाप्तिः B_4] समाप्ति $Ś_1$ 21 प्रपञ्चः $Ś_1$] प्राचः B_4 22 तादृग् B_4] दृग् $Ś_1$ 23 अथ च मन B_4] अच मन $Ś_1$

---

23 मन एव] *Bhagavadgītā* 6.5

चेद्ग्रन्थादावुपनिबन्धनं किंप्रयोजनायेत्यत आह धीराणामिति संशयविपर्ययरहिता धीर्येषां ते धीरास्तेषामनुगणनाय दृढीकरणायेत्यर्थः । यथा तेऽपि मङ्गलकरणपूर्वकमेव ग्रन्थारम्भं स्वीकुर्युरिति ननु पूर्वाचार्यैः कृतानां मङ्गलानां उच्छिष्टभक्षणमिव पुनरारम्भोऽनुचित इत्याह स्वरचितपद्ययुग्मकेनेति स्वेन आत्मना रचितं यत्पद्ययुग्मं तेनेत्यर्थः एतेन पूर्वाचार्यकृतमङ्गलपरिग्रहशङ्का परिहृतेति । यथा युग्मेत्युक्तं तथाग्रे वक्ष्यतीति

हरतु मनोमलं हरशरीरहरार्धगती
रचयतु पादगं पुलकितं भजतां च शिरः ।
नयनयनाकृतिं विनयता नयतून्नयता-
मतिमतिबुद्धिमर्पयतु पञ्चमुखी सुतराम् ॥

हरस्य शरीरं हरशरीरं शिवस्वरूपं बिन्दुः हरार्धं त्रिकोणं तत्र गतिर्यस्याः । अत्र हरार्धशब्देन अधोमुखत्रिकोणात्मिका शक्तिरुच्यते इति तन्त्रप्रसिद्धम् । तदुक्तं श्रीशङ्करानन्दपादैः

मुखं बिन्दुं कृत्वा कुचयुगमधस्तस्य तदधो
हरार्धं ध्यायेद्यो हरमहिषि ते मन्मथकलां ।
स सद्यः सङ्क्षोभं नयति वनिताम् इत्यतिलघु
त्रिलोकीमप्याशु भ्रमयति रवीन्दुस्तनयुगाम् ॥

इति । शिवदृष्टावपि अहं बिन्दुर्विसर्गस्त्वमित्युक्तेः तथा चास्या यन्त्रोद्धारः

बिन्दुत्रिकोणवसुकोणदशारवृत्त-
नागाश्रषोडशदलाख्यशरच्चरित्रम्
भूमन्दिरत्रयमिदं परमार्थयन्त्रं

---

1 संशय B4] संशयं Ś1 3 आरम्भो Ś1] आम्भो B4 4 युग्मं Ś1] युगं B4 5 वक्ष्यतीति B4] वक्ष्यतेति Ś1 7 पादगं B4] पानगं Ś1 9 मुखी सुतराम् Ś1] मुखीमुत्तराम् B4 10 हरस्य B4] हरस Ś1 11 पादैः Ś1] स्वामिपादैः B4 12 बिन्दुं Ś1] बिन्दु B4 13 ध्यायेद् B4] ध्ययेद् Ś1 14 वनिताम् coni.] वनिता Ś1B4 14 अतिलघु Ś1] उतिलघु B4 15 युगाम् Ś1] युगम् B4 17 वसु Ś1] वस्तु B4

---

15 मुखं बिन्दुं] *Saundaryalaharī* 19 16 अहं बिन्दुर्विसर्गस्त्वम्] quotation untraced

सर्वार्थसाधनकरं परमार्थदेव्या ॥

इति यद्वाहश्चरश्च हरौ शश्चरश्च शरौ तयोरवयवतया ईरीकारः द्वन्द्वान्ते श्रूयमाणस्य शब्दस्य प्रत्येकमभिसम्बध्यमानत्वात् ह्रीश्रीति सिद्धम् । कीदृक् अहरार्धगतिः अहरोऽनुस्वारः तदर्ध-मनुनासिकः तेन गतिर्ज्ञानं यस्य ईदृशी सार्थात् ह्रीं श्रींस्वरूपेत्यर्थः । श्रीश्वरीपक्षेऽपि हरस्य शिवस्य शरीरं हरशरीरं तत् हरति इति हरशरीरहरा । अर्धं गतेरर्धगतिः अर्धस्वरूपं अर्ध-पिप्पल्यादित्वात्समासः हरशरीरहरा अर्धगतिरर्धस्वरूपं यस्याः शिवयोरर्धनारीश्वरत्वादिति उभयोरेवाभेदाध्यवसानादीश्वरीस्वरूपमपि निर्णीतम् । तदुक्तं रुद्रयामले

बाला च तरुणी प्रौढा महाविद्या सरस्वती ।
पञ्चविद्यात्मिका देवी गायत्री परिकल्पिता ॥

ब्रह्मा विष्णुश्च रुद्रश्च ईश्वरश्च सदाशिवः ।
पञ्चब्रह्मात्मिका प्रोक्ता गायत्री मोक्षदायिनी ॥

ईदृशी पञ्चमुखी गायत्री पञ्चमुखः शिवस्तस्य स्त्रीः । पञ्चमुखी ईश्वरी च मनोमलं मन-सोऽन्तःकरणस्य तदुपासनरूपं मोहं हरतु दूरीकरोत्वित्यर्थः इत्यनेनाशीर्वादना द्योत्यते । अथ च प्रणमतां भज भजतां भक्तानामस्मदादीनां पदयोर्गतं शिरोऽनुग्रहजन्यकरस्पर्शादिभिः पुलकितं रचयतु संजातपुलकं करोतु इत्यर्थः एतेन नतिर्द्योत्यते । अथ च नयनयनाकृतिं नयनयनानां नयचक्षुषां आ साकल्येण कृतिं राज्यं उन्नयतां वृद्धिं नयतु प्रापयतु इत्यर्थः । एतेन वस्तुनिर्देशः राजरूपवस्तुनिर्देशो हि ग्रन्थादौ श्रेयान् यथा नैषधीयकाव्ये श्रीहर्षक-विना राजनिर्देशेनैव वस्तुरूपमङ्गलं स्वीकृतम् । कथम्भूता पञ्चमुखी त्रिनयना प्रत्येकं मुखेषु त्रिनयनत्वात्पञ्चदशनयनेत्यर्थः । तथा च सुतरामतिशयेन अतिमति मतिमतिक्रम्य बुद्धिगो-चरं यथा न स्यात्तथा बुद्धिं सम्पत्तिमर्पयतु प्रयच्छत्विति श्लोकार्थः अलं तावन्मङ्गलाचरणे बहुविस्तरेण । इदानीं प्रकृतमेवानुसरामः ॥

---

3 सम्बध्यमान coni.] सम्बध्यमात $Ś_1$, सम्बधामान B_4 3 गतिः B_4] गति $Ś_1$ 6 आदित्वात् B_4] आदित्वा $Ś_1$ 6 यस्याः B_4] यस्या $Ś_1$ 9 विद्यात्मिका देवी $Ś_1$] विद्यत्मिका देवि B_4 9 परिकल्पिता $Ś_1$] परिकीर्तिता B_4 12 मलं B_4] चलं $Ś_1$ 13 अनेनाशीर्वादना $Ś_1$] एनां आशीर्वादता B_4 14 भज भजतां $Ś_1$] भवता B_4 16 कृतिं B_4] कृति $Ś_1$ 18 नैव B_4] नैवं $Ś_1$

---

1 बिन्दुत्रिकोण] The verse combines several fragments of frequently quoted verses, see, for instance, *Devīrahasya* 10.17. 3 अहर-] unclear, since the text commented upon reads *harārdhagati.*

स्वातन्त्र्यतन्त्रं स्वात्मान्तर्भावैकनिपुणं परम्
परस्थं स्वपरात्मानं संस्तौमि स्वमहेश्वरम् ॥

कृतकल्पवृक्षबन्धे तीर्थ्यानुग्राह्यनोदनावशितैः
साहिबकौलपदस्थैर्विरच्यते स्वल्पतात्पर्यम् ॥

तत्र तावत्पूर्वोक्तानां तिसृणामेव महादृष्टीनामद्वैतप्रतिपादनमेव परमार्थः । किन्तु कुत्रापि स्वस्वदर्शनार्थदर्शनविशेषोऽपि प्रतिपादितः तद्विशेषविरोधपरिहारार्थमेवास्य यत्नस्य कृतकृत्यतेति विचार्य तत्तात्पर्यमग्रे स्फुटीकुर्मः इति ॥

[Commentary on the first prose section]

तत्रादौ श्रीमच्छ्रीसुस्वतन्त्रेत्यादिरुपोद्घातः । अत्रायमर्थः । त्वं प्रत्यभिज्ञया स्वसम्मुखीनः सदा सन्निहितश्च । अयं स्वानुभवसमसमयमेव साक्षात्कृतः । त्वमयमित्यनेनाहमिति परमार्थः । यथा वारस्थाः वारं वारं पारं च पारं वदन्ति तत्पारस्थाश्च तेषां वारं पारं तेषां पारं च वारं वदन्ति । यथा चैक एव मानवः पितुः पुत्रः पुत्रस्य पिता जामातुः श्वशुरः श्वशुरस्य च जामाता इत्येवमादिसम्बन्धमयोऽप्येक एव ।

तथा त्वमहमिति पदयोः परस्परपर्यायत्वं सिद्धं । स्वस्य स्वस्मिन्नहमिति प्रत्ययात्परस्मिंश्च त्वमिति प्रत्ययात्परस्य च तत्प्रोक्तत्वं प्रत्ययवतः स्वेनाहमित्यनुसन्धानात्तस्य च परेण त्वमिति वचनप्रतिपादनात् ।

एतदेव निर्णीतं वासिष्ठे योगे त्वमहमिति शब्दाभ्यामित्यादिना । परमशिवः परा मा मोक्षलक्ष्मीर्यस्य स परमः । पिपर्ति स्वाहन्तारसेन स्वातन्त्र्यरूपमनाश्रितादिमहीपर्यन्तं वि-

---

3 आनुग्राह्य B_4] आनुग्रह्य Ś$_1$ 4 विरच्यते B_4] विरचिते Ś$_1$ 4 स्वल्प B_4] स्वस्वल्प Ś$_1$ 5 कुत्रापि Ś$_1$Ś$_2$] कुत्रापि कुत्रापि B_4 6 अस्य Ś$_2$] अद्य Ś$_1$$B_4$ 7 विचार्य Ś$_1$] विचार्थ B_4 7 तत्तात्पर्यम् Ś$_1$] तत्रान्यर्यम् B_4 8 तत्रादौ] B_4 reads the complete mūla-text concluding with इत्यन्तं प्रथमोपोद्घातः 8 प्रत्यभिज्ञया B_4G_2Ś$_2$] प्रत्यभिज्ञाया Ś$_1$ 9 इति G_2Ś$_2$Ś$_1$] इति सर्वानुभवसिद्धः B_4 11 श्वशुरः B_4G_2Ś$_1$] श्वशुर Ś$_2$ 13 सिद्धं] om. G_2Ś$_2$ 14 परस्मिंश्च त्वमिति प्रत्ययात् G_2] om. B_4Ś$_1$Ś$_2$ 14 तस्य G_2Ś$_1$Ś$_2$] परस्मिंश्च त्वमित्यनुसन्धानात्तस्य B_1 16 निर्णीतं Ś$_1$$B_4$] निर्णीतं च G_2Ś$_2$ 16 योगे G_2] योगशास्त्रे Ś$_1$Ś$_2$$B_4$ 16 आदिना G_2Ś$_1$] आदि श्लोकसप्तकेन B_4, आदि Ś$_2$ 16 परा मा coni.] परमा Ś$_2$, परा Ś$_1$$B_4G_2$

श्वविभवं पूरयति परः। तदेव सृष्ट्वा तदेवानुप्राविक्षदित्यादि। अनेन जीवात्मनानुप्रविश्येत्यादि तस्माद्वा एतस्मादात्मन आकाशः सम्भूत इत्यादि च श्रुतेः

भोक्तैव भोग्यभावेन सदा सर्वत्र संस्थितः।

इति शैवश्रुतेश्च।

सदाशिवात्मना वेद्मि स वा वेत्ति मदात्मना।

इति श्रीमहागुरुश्रीसोमानन्दपादोक्तेश्च।

पिपर्ति तदेव पालयति स्वस्वरूपमयं स्वात्मना स्वात्मनि स्वत आविर्भाव्य स्वरूपानुसन्धानेन कचत्प्रकाशविमर्शमयं विदधातीति वा परः। माति प्रमाति स्वतन्त्रकर्तृतया स्वस्वरूपाभेदमयमेतदेव स्वात्मनि स्वात्मना विमृशतीति सः। परश्चासौ मश्च परमः। इन्द्रियेभ्यः परो ह्यर्था इत्यादिश्रुत्या वा निर्णीतः। परः स चासौ मश्चेति वा। अथ च परं द्वितीयं मिनोति प्रक्षिपति दूरीकरोति परमः अद्वितीयः। परं देहेन्द्रियादि मीनाति। अनुभवसमये हिनस्तीति वा परमः। परं देहादिं मयते स्वाज्ञानसमये विनिमयते स्वात्माभिमानत्वेन व्यतिहरतीति वा परमः। परं परनादं मिमीति निदिध्यासनावसरे शब्दयति स्वविमर्शपात्रतामापादयतीति वा परमः। अथ च रहस्याद्वयदृष्ट्या पर उत्तमश्चासौ मः सचेतनो मकारः मकारस्य चेतनाचेतनत्वेन द्विविधत्वात्पवर्गान्त्यो चेतनो मकारः पञ्चदशस्वरानुस्वाररूपस्तु सचेतनः बिन्दुरित्यर्थः

स एव परमः शिवः।

अहं बिन्दुर्विसर्गस्त्वम्

---

1 second hand writing Śāradā from तदेव in B$_4$ 1 अनुप्राविक्षद् Ś$_2$] अनुप्रविश्येत्यादि G$_2$, अनुप्राविष्यद् B$_4$, illegible Ś$_1$ 1 जीवात्मना Ś$_1$] जीवेनात्मना G$_2$B$_4$Ś$_2$ 2 तस्माद्वा G$_2$Ś$_1$B$_4$] तस्मा Ś$_2$ 2 श्रुतेः B$_4$G$_2$Ś$_2$] श्रुतिवचनात् Ś$_1$ 8 माति G$_2$B$_4$Ś$_2$] ति Ś$_1$ 8 कर्तृतया B$_4$G$_2$] कर्तृकतया Ś$_2$, तृतया Ś$_1$ 9 स्वात्मना] om. Ś$_2$ 10 ह्यर्था G$_2$B$_4$Ś$_1$] ह्यर्थ Ś$_2$ 10 परः स G$_2$B$_4$Ś$_2$] परा Ś$_1$ 13 परनादं G$_2$B$_4$] परानादं Ś$_1$Ś$_2$ 13 निधि] om. Ś$_2$ 15 चेतनाचेतनत्वेन G$_2$B$_4$Ś$_2$] चेतनताचेतनत्वेन Ś$_1$ 16 अनुस्वार G$_2$Ś$_2$] अनुसार Ś$_1$B$_4$

---

1 तदेव सृष्ट्वा] *Taittirīyopaniṣad* 2.6 2 अनेन जीवात्मना] *Chāndogyopaniṣad* 6.3 2 तस्माद्वा एतस्माद्] *Taittirīyopaniṣad* 2.1 3 भोक्तैव] *Spandakārikā* 3.2 5 सदाशिवात्मना] *Śivadṛṣṭi* 5.106 10 इन्द्रियेभ्यः परा] *Kaṭhopaniṣad* 3.10

इति शिवसूक्तेः। अनुत्तरशिवाहन्तापरामर्शसार इत्यर्थः शिवः शमशेषोपद्रवरहितं। एतस्यैवानन्दस्यान्यान्यानन्दानि मात्रामुपजीवयन्तीति को ह्येवान्यात्कः प्राण्याद्यद्येष आनन्दस्य मीमांसा न स्यादिति रसो वै स इत्यादि च श्रुतेः वित्तसुताद्यन्यानन्दव्यतिरिक्तं चैतन्यानन्दलक्षणं कल्याणं वाति राति ददाति स्वकल्पितमोहापसरणमात्रेण स्वाभिन्नानुग्राह्येभ्य आविष्करोतीति शिवः। परमश्चासौ शिवश्च परमशिवः। जयसि सर्वोत्कृष्टत्वेन वर्तसे। यः किल सर्वोत्कृष्टः स सर्वनमस्योऽपि भवति। यथा पथि प्रचलतो राजादेः सर्वोत्कृष्टस्य नमस्काराकरणे स्वस्यैव खण्डनोन्मत्तप्रायता वा। न तु तस्य कापि क्षतिरिति तं स्वात्ममहेश्वरं प्रति प्रणताः स्म इति सर्वत्रैव जयत्यादीनामियमेव वर्तनी। नन्वद्वैतनये नमस्कार्याद्यनवशेषे नमस्कारकरणं कथं कस्य केन वा घटते द्वैतापत्तेरिति चेत्। सत्यम्। किन्तु णम प्रह्वत्वे इति धातोरर्थानुगमाद्देहाद्यभिमानप्राधान्यमधस्पदीकृत्य तन्मयसमावेशापन्नाः स्म इति नमस्कारकरणाकूटम्।

अयं त्वं कथंभूतः। श्रीमांश्चासौ श्रीरेव च स्वस्वतन्त्रश्चासौ अनाश्रितश्चासौ निर्भागश्चासौ परमप्रकाशविमर्शमयपारमैश्वर्यानुभावानुभावुकप्रथितमहितनिजसहजपरमानन्दाद्वयसत्तासामान्यस्पन्दश्च सः। श्रीः शक्तिः शोभाज्ञानसंकोचदौर्गत्यहारिणी परमलक्ष्मीश्च विद्यते यस्यासौ। ता एव भूमा यस्य च सः। ता एव प्रशंसा यस्यासौ च। ता एव नित्ययोगो यस्यासौ च। श्रीमान् श्रीयं संसाराख्यां शोभां मश्नातीति श्रीमत्। स चासाविति वा संसारस्य शोभारूपत्वं स्वकल्पिताज्ञानकाले भासमानत्वात्सः स्वयं श्रीश्च तत्त्रितयरूपः। सुष्ठु स्वतन्त्रः। अभेदे भेत्ता भेदिते चान्तरनुसन्धानेनाभेत्ता च। अनन्यमुखप्रेक्षी निःसचिवमहाराज्यसंभारभर्तेति यावत्। अत एवानाश्रितः। षड्रूपप्रमातृकालासु वर्तमानोऽपि ता अतीत्य सदा स्थितः। अत एव निर्भागश्च। न ह्यनाश्रितस्य भागकरणमुपपद्यते। तस्य विभाजितस्य स्वस्यैव खण्डनापत्तेः।

को ददर्श प्रथमं जायमानमस्थन्वन्तं यदनस्था बिभर्तीत्यादिश्रुतेः।

---

1 शमशेषो $G_2 B_4^{pc}$ $\acute{S}_2$] शममेषो $\acute{S}_1$, शशेषो B_4^{ac} 1 उपद्रव $G_2\acute{S}_2$] उपद्धव $B_4\acute{S}_1$ 2 प्राण्याद्य $G_2\acute{S}_2$] प्राणाद्य $\acute{S}_1 B_4$ 5 सर्वोत्कृष्टत्वेन $\acute{S}_1\acute{S}_2 G_2$] सर्वोत्कृष्टेन B_4 7 नमस्काराकरणे $G_2\acute{S}_2$] नमस्कार्करणे $\acute{S}_1 B_4$ 7 खण्डनोन्मत्त $G_2 B_4$] खण्डनोन्मत्ता $\acute{S}_2$, खण्डोन्मत्त $\acute{S}_1$ 8 जयत्यादीनाम् $G_2\acute{S}_2$] इत्यादीनाम् B_4, जयत्यादिनाम् $\acute{S}_1$ 8 नमस्कार्या $G_2\acute{S}_2$] नमस्कारा $\acute{S}_1 B_4$ 14 श्रीः $G_2 B_4\acute{S}_2$] श्री $\acute{S}_1$ 14 दौर्गत्य $G_2 B_4\acute{S}_2$] दौर्गति $\acute{S}_1$ 17 स्वकल्पिताज्ञान $G_2 B_4\acute{S}_2$] स्वकल्पितज्ञान $\acute{S}_1$ 19 कलासु $G_2\acute{S}_2$] कालासु $\acute{S}_1 B_4$

---

2 एतस्यैवानन्दस्यान्यान्यानन्दानि मात्रामुपजीवयन्ति] adaptation of *Bṛhadāraṇyakopaniṣad* 4.3.32, where we read *bhūtāni* for *ānandāni*. 3 को ह्येवान्यात् [...] वै स] *Taittirīyopaniṣad* 2.7,8 22 को ददर्श] *Ṛgveda* 1.164.4

स्वपदा स्वशिरश्छायां यद्वल्लङ्घितुमीहते ।
पादोद्देशे शिरो न स्यात्तथेयं बैन्दवी कला ॥

इति रहस्योक्तेश्च । अत एव परमप्रकाशविमर्शमयं यत्पारमैश्वर्यं तस्यानुभावः । महत्त्वं तस्य ये अनुभावुकाः । तदनुभवकारिणः । तेषु तेषां वा प्रथितः । प्रकटीकृतो महितो वृद्धः पूजितश्च निजो नित्यः स्वश्च सहजः स्वाभिन्नः प्राङ्निर्णीतपरमानन्दाद्वयसत्तासामान्यस्पन्दो येन स च । ननु परमशिव इत्यस्यैव विशेष्यस्य विवेके कृते एतानि श्रीमदित्यादीनि विशेषणानि स्वयमेवार्थायातानि । अर्थायातेषु च तेषु पुनस्तत्प्रतिपादनेऽग्रतोऽन्यशेषवाक्यप्रतिपादने च पौनरुक्त्यप्रसङ्ग इति चेत् । न । यत एक एव स स्वात्ममहेश्वरो निर्वृतैः संवादशतैर्महद्भिः प्रतिपाद्यमानः स्वानुग्रहशक्तिवतां कथं कथमपि साक्षाद्भावमायातीति । पुनः पुनस्तदेव ब्रह्मतत्त्वं निगमादिभिः प्रतिपादितमनन्तशक्तिस्वरूपत्वाच्च बहुधा निर्णेष्यमाणं विचारपदवीमारोहति नानाजन्मकोटिलग्नमलापसरणकारकं च भवतीत्यत एकः पुनः पुनः प्रतिपादितः प्रतिपादनीयोऽपि न पौनरुक्त्यमावहति । अत एव चैतैर्विशेषणैर्बार्हस्पत्यादिवादानां प्रतिक्षेपः । यतः यत्किञ्चित्प्रकाशमयं तत्तत्तानतीतं स्वस्वरूपमेव यच्चाप्रकाशं तत्स्वयमेवासत्तामापाद्यमानं परस्य किञ्चित्कर्तुमक्षमम् । अत एव गीतं श्रीप्रत्यभिज्ञायां कर्तरि ज्ञातरीत्यादितत्तद्वादानां निराकरणं चाग्रत एव स्फुटीभविष्यतीति नाधिकमिहोन्मील्यते ।

पुनः किंभूतः । उदितोदितं नितरामुदितं । उत्क्रान्तं इतं गमनं येन च सर्वव्यापकत्वात् । उच्चैरितं ज्ञानं च यस्य । उदितं सततोदितं सृष्ट्यादिभावविकलं स्वाभिन्नपरमशक्तिसाम्राज्यं यस्य । न हि परमः शिवो निःशक्तिः कदाचिदपि भवति निःशक्तिमत्त्वे सर्गादीनामप्रतिष्ठानात् । न च सदा शक्तिमत्त्वे सर्गादीनां सततं सद्भावेन मोक्षानवाप्तिशङ्केति वाच्यं सर्गादिषु सत्स्वपि तस्य सदैव सर्वभावानां स्वात्मभावाकलनेन बन्धानापत्तेः । असत्स्वपि च तेषु परशक्तावेव स्वरूपसंकलनेन शक्तिशक्तिमतोरभेदावभासात् ।

---

4 प्रकटीकृतो coni.] प्रकटीवतो G$_2$B$_4$Ś$_1$Ś$_2$ 4 महितो G$_2$Ś$_2$] सहितो B$_4$Ś$_1$ 6 च] om. B$_4$ 8 पादने G$_2$Ś$_1$Ś$_2$] पादनेन B$_4$ 13 बार्हस्पत्य] note in G$_2$ चार्वाक 13 तत्तत्तानतीतं G$_2$B$_4$Ś$_2$] तत्ततानन्नीतं Ś$_1$ 14 तत् G$_2$B$_4$Ś$_2$] तत्तत् Ś$_1$ 18 च G$_2$B$_4$Ś$_2$] स Ś$_1$ 19 शक्तिमत्त्वे G$_2$Ś$_2$] शक्तिमत्ते B$_4$Ś$_1$ 21 भावा G$_2$B$_4$Ś$_2$] भा Ś$_1$ 22 मतोर् G$_2$B$_4$Ś$_2$] मतेर् Ś$_1$

---

2 स्वपदा] quoted in *Pratyabhijñāhṛdaya 1* as from the *Trikasāra* 15 कर्तरि] *Īśvarapratyabhijñākārikā* 1.1.2

पुनः किंभूतः। राजेति। राजानो मनोबुद्धिजीवादयः। तेषां राजानो महाजीवा ईशसदाशिवत्वाद्यभिमानिनस्तेषामीश्वरः। यतस्तेऽपि तदीयप्रकाशविमर्शमयपरविभवविप्रुषामवाप्या परमेश्वराः संवृताः। किमुच्यते। स सर्वमहेश्वरः। स्वयं स्वस्मिन्स्वस्य प्रकाशस्यानुसन्धाता सद्रूपविमर्शविषदः। प्रकाशस्य च विमर्शत्वं स्वयमापन्नं। इतरप्रकाशवैलक्षण्येन श्रुत्यादिप्रतिपादितस्वयंप्रकाशानुसन्धानाद्विमर्शानापन्नश्च प्रकाशोऽकिञ्चित्करत्वादप्रकाश एव। अथ चाप्रकाशोऽपि प्रकाश एव तस्याप्यप्रकाशत्वेन प्रकाशनात्। प्रकाशं विनाप्रकाशत्वाख्यधर्मस्याप्यनवभासात्। अज्ञानमपि ज्ञानमेव तस्याप्यज्ञानभावेन ज्ञेयत्वाज्ज्ञानाव्यतिरेकात्॥

---

2 आद्यभिमानिन $G_2B_4\acute{S}_2$] आदिभिमानिव $\acute{S}_1$ 5 सन्धानात् $G_2B_4\acute{S}_2$] सन्धात् $\acute{S}_1$ 6 ऽकिञ्चित्कर $\acute{S}_2$] किञ्चिदकिञ्चित्कर $\acute{S}_1G_2B_4$ 7 अज्ञानभावेन $G_2\acute{S}_2$] अज्ञभावेन $\acute{S}_1B_4$ 8 ज्ञानाव्यतिरेकात् $G_2\acute{S}_2$] ज्ञानव्यतिरेकात् $B_4\acute{S}_1$

[mūla text, second section]

ओं अस्यैव ते स्वातन्त्र्ये विवर्तमानस्य सा परमसहजाहन्ताविशेषशेषा शेषसंभारभरणादिबीजभूता त्रिशूलाकारपश्यन्त्यादित्रयविमर्शसखानन्तशक्तिमणिप्रभासमुद्भेदसामरस्यमयी चिदेकैवैषा काचनानन्तानुत्तरनिरुत्तरसर्वोत्तरस्वविलासभासकत्वत उत्तीर्णा त्रिकमयैक्यपरसहजौजोविषदा सदोत्तुङ्गाभङ्गपरहर्षस्पन्दोदयोद्यता तत्तन्माहेश्वरनानाशक्तिनिमेषसमुन्मेषोन्मेषनिमेषतत्त्वोन्मिषितातीव सर्वातीतापि सर्वैव समुज्जृम्भमाणा महाशक्तिः पराख्या ॥

[commentary]

अस्यैव ते पूर्वनिर्णीतस्य परमशिवस्य सा प्रक्रान्तपरमशिवाभेदसारत्वात् प्रक्रान्ता तद्वदेव ज्ञानिषु विपरीतेषु च प्रसिद्धत्वात्प्रसिद्धा ज्ञानिभिर्विपरीतैश्च क्रमेण विदिताविदितदृष्ट्या चानुभूता ।

ननु ज्ञानिनां विदितेति तैरनुभूता विपरीतैश्चाविदितत्वात्कथमनुभूतेति चेत् । उच्यते । अहं तं तां वा न जानामि इतिवदन्नज्ञान्यपि जानात्येव अहंपदविमर्शाभिन्नत्वेन प्रकाशमानत्वात् । किन्तु ज्ञानी यथाभूतमनुभवति । अज्ञानी च देहाद्यभिमानित्वेन विपर्ययेण जानन्नपि जानात्येव । तस्या अखण्डप्रकाशत्वेन सर्वाभेदसारत्वात् । तत्स्वरूपहानेनाहं जानामीत्येवादिविमर्शस्यापि विमर्शमयत्वेनान्यथानुपपत्तेः । एषा त्वदभिन्नत्वेनानुभूतचरा पराख्या परा एकस्यास्त्वदभिन्नाया अपि चन्द्रचन्द्रिकादिवद् द्वितीया आख्या आह्वानं यस्याः परवत्परमेश्वरवदा समन्तात् ख्या प्रथनं यस्याश्च । परः परमेश्वर एव आख्या नाम यस्याश्च । परेभ्यो महाजीवेभ्यः सकाशात् आख्या प्रथनं यस्याश्च । परं परमात्मानं निर्णीता सती आख्याति आविष्करोतीति च । परा अपराभिन्ना आख्या नामानि यस्याश्च । यानि कानिचन नामानि महद्भिस्तस्या विहितानि तानि सर्वाणि न तदर्थप्रतिपादकानि किन्तु व्यवहारमात्रार्थमेव

---

1 ओं cett.] om. C_{1-3} 1 ते cett.] om. C_{1-3} 2 आदि] आदिं C_2 3 चिदेकैवैषा $\acute{S}_2 B_3$] चिदेवेकैवैषा C_{1-3} 3 निरुत्तर] om. $\acute{S}_2$ 4 कत्वत $B_3 \acute{S}_2$] त्वं तत C_{1-3} 4 उत्तीर्णा $B_3 \acute{S}_2$] उत्तीर्ण C_{1-3} 4 मयैक्यपर $B_3 \acute{S}_2$] मयैक्यपरम C_{1-3} 4 सदोत्तुङ्गा $C_1 G_2 \acute{S}_2$] मदोत्तङ्गा $\acute{S}_1$ सदोत्तुगा $C_2 C_3$ 4 भङ्गपर $B_3 \acute{S}_2 C_1 C_3$] भङ्गपरम C_2 7 ते] om. $\acute{S}_1$ 7 परमशिवस्य $\acute{S}_1 G_2 B_4$] पारमशिवस्य $\acute{S}_2$ 8 प्रसिद्धत्वात्प्रसिद्धा $G_2 \acute{S}_1 \acute{S}_2$] प्रसिद्धात्प्रसिद्धात् B_4 10 विपरीतैश्चा $G_2 B_4 \acute{S}_2$] विपरीतश्चा $\acute{S}_1$ 14 उपपत्तेः $G_2 B_4 \acute{S}_2$] उपत्तेः $\acute{S}_1$

कल्पितानि निर्नामत्वादिति भावः ।

अत एव महाशक्तिः महती सर्वोत्तमा सा चासौ शक्तिः महाशक्तिः स्वाभिन्नस्वविभव सामर्थ्यं महती चासौ अशक्तिः नशक्तिः किन्तु शिव एवेति च रहस्यदृष्ट्या च स्वनिमेषतः स्वविभवोन्मेषेण अहमिति पराहन्तापरामर्शः तस्यैव परामर्शस्य च स्वविभवनिमेषावसरे स्वोन्मुखताख्यस्वोन्मेषेन व्यत्ययतः महा इति च परामर्शः । सा चासौ शक्तिः ।

अत्र च शब्दसृष्टिविवेकेन अकारहकारयोराद्यन्तयोः सर्वान्त्यविसर्गसमुदायेनानुस्वारापत्त्या अहमिति परामर्शः । ननु अकाराकारयोः शब्दशासनदृष्ट्या सन्निहितत्वमपरदृष्ट्या च वर्गादिरकारस्य वर्गादीनां कादीनां च वा सन्निहितत्वं परस्परमुचितम् । नकारहकारयोराद्यन्तभावेनाद्यन्तदूरतयावभासादिति चेत् । सत्यम् । किन्तु अत्राकारहकारयोरेव सन्निहितत्वं परस्परसमुदायित्वं चोचितं । मातृकायाः पञ्चाशदक्षरमय्या मालात्वेन भासमानत्वात् । तथाहि मालाया मादेर्मणेर्द्वितीयस्यान्यस्य वा न तथा संयुक्तत्वम् । यथाद्यस्यान्त्यस्य च । अतोऽकारहकारयोरेवाश्लेषविधिना नितरां सन्निहितत्वं नान्यवर्णैः सहादिवर्णस्य सन्निहितत्वम् । एतयोः समुदाय एव चाहमिति परामर्शः । अहमेवाग्र आसं सदेवेदमग्र आसीदित्यादिश्रुतिशासनात् । विमर्शः सोऽहमित्ययमिति प्रत्यभिज्ञाशासनाच्च पराया एव च स्वौन्मुख्यहानेन शिवौन्मुख्यमेव महा इति परामर्शमहालयः । स एव च स्वपदानुसन्धानं महा इति शक्तिः परशिवात्मिकैव भवति पूर्वानुवर्तनेन जयति वा अत्रैवास्यते । इति सम्बन्धषष्ठ्यप्यमुमेव सम्बन्धं शिवशक्त्योराविष्करोति चेतनस्य भावश्चैतन्यमिति शिवसूत्रविमर्शिन्युक्तेः । राहोः शिरः केतोः पुच्छ इत्यादिवत् । न तु पितुः पुत्र इत्यादिवत् ।

अस्यैव ते कथंभूतस्य स्वातन्त्र्ये पूर्वोक्तस्वनिर्मितस्वाभिन्नस्वविभवे विवर्तमानस्य विवर्तेन रज्जुसर्पादिदृष्टान्तवत्स्वकल्पितमोहावृतमतीनां भासमानस्य । अयमेव च ब्रह्माद्वयशिवाद्वयदृष्ट्योरन्योन्यं स्वस्वविशिष्ठार्थः । यद्ब्रह्माद्वयवादिभिर्विवर्तवादो निर्णीतः शिवाद्वय-

---

2 चासौ Ś$_2$G$_2$B$_4$] सा चासौ Ś$_1$ 2 महाशक्तिः] om. Ś$_2$ 2 स्वविभव G$_2$Ś$_1$Ś$_2$] स्वस्वविभव B$_4$ 3 अशक्तिः नशक्तिः G$_2$Ś$_1$Ś$_2$] अशक्तिन शाक्ते B$_4$ 6 अत्र G$_2$Ś$_1$Ś$_2$] अत B$_4$ 6 आनुस्वारा G$_2$B$_4$Ś$_2$] आनुसारा Ś$_1$ 7 शब्दशासन G$_2$B$_4$Ś$_2$] शब्दशासनयोः Ś$_1$ 9 एव G$_2$B$_4$Ś$_2$] आद्यन्तरेव Ś$_1$ 10 चोचितं G$_2$B$_4$Ś$_2$] चोदितं Ś$_1$ 11 संयुक्तत्वम् G$_2$Ś$_2$] संयुक्तम् B$_4$Ś$_1$ 13 समुदाय G$_2$B$_4$Ś$_2$] समुय Ś$_1$ 13 परामर्शः G$_2$Ś$_1$] परापरामर्शः B$_4$Ś$_2$ 13 एवाग्र G$_2$B$_4$Ś$_2$] एग्र Ś$_1$ 15 स्वौन्मुख्य G$_2$Ś$_2$] सौन्मुख्य Ś$_1$B$_4$ 18 उक्तेः G$_2$Ś$_2$] उक्तैः Ś$_1$B$_4$ 19 स्वातन्त्र्ये G$_2$B$_4$Ś$_2$] स्वातन्त्र्यै Ś$_1$ 20 विवर्तन B$_4$G$_2$Ś$_2$] विवर्तनेन Ś$_1$ 21 दृष्ट्यो–शिवाद्वय] om. Ś$_1$B$_4$

---

9 अवभासादिति] Ś$_1$ inserts four folios with a different text here. 18 चेतनस्य भावश्चैतन्यम्] *Śivasūtravimarśī* ad 1.1

वादिभिश्च स्वातन्त्र्यवादः। तयोरनेन वाक्येनैक्यप्रतिपादनमस्माभिराविष्कृतम्। यथा न विवर्तः केनचिदन्येन पदार्थेन तस्य महेश्वरस्य किन्तु स्वकीयं स्वातन्त्र्यरूपं विभवमुन्मील्य तस्मिन्नेव स्वयं विवर्ततया स्वकल्पितावरणवतां भासते। स्वानुग्रहवतां च तदपसरणेन यथास्थितो भ्रमादिभेदबुद्धिमपहाय स्वप्रकाशविमर्शमय एव भासतेतराम्। न हि परमेश्वरस्य केनचन भिन्नत्वं येनान्येनान्यस्येव तस्य विवर्तरूपो भ्रमो भासेत स्वयं स्वप्रकाशविमर्शसारत्वात्। सर्वथा विवर्तमपहाय स्वानुग्रहशक्त्यानुग्राह्याणां शुद्धबुद्धमुक्तपरमानन्दाद्वयस्वभावं ब्रह्मैकमेव प्रतिभाति। स्वातन्त्र्यमतिं चापहाय स एक एवानाश्रितः स्वतन्त्रो भासते इति न कोऽपि विरोधः। उभयोरपि परमार्थत ऐक्यप्रतिपादन एव प्रयोगात्। एवमग्रेऽपि तयोः स्वस्वविशेषपरिहानौ परस्परमभिन्नतासमन्वयेयमेवाभिप्रायः।

सा कथंभूता परमसहजाहन्ताविशेषशेषा परमा चासौ सहजा च या अहन्ता तस्या यो विशेषः स एव शेषो यस्याः। अथ वा परमा चासौ सहजा च परमा परात्वेन सहजा च शिवाभिन्नत्वेन।

पुनः किंभूता अहन्ताविशेषः उत्तमाहन्ता। अहन्ताया उत्तममध्यमाधमरूपत्वात्। स एव शेषो यस्याः। सर्वस्येदन्तादेः सुषुप्तादिदशायां प्रलयदशायां वा विनाशेऽपि स्वाहन्तैव शिष्यते इत्यर्थः। अथ च अहन्तैव विशेषः। विगतशेषः शेषो यस्याः शेषस्यापि शेषभावो यत्रेति तात्पर्यम्। अथ च विगतशेषश्चासौ शेषः शेषादिभावविकलः शेषः स चाहन्तैव तस्याः अथ च शेषाणां शेषः शेषशेषः विगतः शेषशेषः विशेषशेषः। अहन्तैव विशेषशेषो यस्याः सा। पुनः किंभूता। अशेषसम्भारभरणादिबीजभूता न शेषः येषां ते अशेषाः।

सदाशिवप्रभृतयस्तेषां सम्यग्भारस्य महत्त्वलक्ष्यार्थस्य परिकरस्य वा। भरणं धारणं तदादौ येषां तेषां बीजभूता बीजमिव। आदिना सर्गप्रलयपिधानानुग्रहाणां ग्रहणं सर्गस्यैव प्रथमं समुचितेऽप्युपादाने। तेषु सर्गादीनामाभासमयत्वादिव स्थितेरेव प्राधान्यात्। प्रथमं तस्या एव ग्रहणं। अथ च अशेषो यः सम्भारः शिवस्यैव स्वादिमहीपर्यन्तः प्रपञ्चः। तस्य भरणे। आदिबीजभूता। अपरापेक्षयान्येषामीश्वरादीनामपि बीजरूपत्वे सत्यपि प्राधान्येन

---

1 अनेन G$_2$B$_4$Ś$_2$] अन्येन Ś$_1$ 2 विवर्तः G$_2$Ś$_2$] विवर्त Ś$_1$B$_4$ 5 आन्यस्येव B$_4$Ś$_2$G$_2$] आन्यस्यैव Ś$_1$ 5 भासेत G$_2$Ś$_2$] भासते Ś$_1$B$_4$ 6 शुद्ध Ś$_1$B$_4$] illegible G$_2$, नित्यशुद्ध Ś$_2$ 8 प्रयोगात्] om. Ś$_1$ 9 परस्परमभिन्नता G$_2$B$_4$Ś$_2$] परस्परभिन्नता Ś$_1$ 11 सहजा च या [...] चासौ सहजा च] om. Ś$_2$ 11 परात्वेन G$_2$Ś$_1$] परत्वेन B$_4$ (repeats the last phrase परमा परात्वेन सहजा च) 14 स्वाहन्तैव G$_2$Ś$_1$Ś$_2$] स्वाहन्तेव B$_4$ 15 अहन्तैव G$_2$Ś$_1$Ś$_2$] अहन्तेव B$_4$ 20 येषां G$_2$B$_4$Ś$_2$] एषां Ś$_1$ 20 बीजभूता] om. Ś$_1$ 21 सर्गादीनाम् G$_2$Ś$_1$B$_4$] सर्गादीम् Ś$_2$ 21 स्थितेरेव B$_4$G$_2$Ś$_2$] स्थितिरेव Ś$_1$ 23 सत्यपि G$_2$B$_4$Ś$_2$] सत्यमपि Ś$_1$

सैव बीजभूतेत्यर्थः। अथ च अशेषाणां सम्भारो गर्भनिवासः सर्ग इति यावत्। तत्र भरणं पोषणं तदादिबीजभूता अत्रार्थे आदिना स्थित्यादीनां ग्रहणं। अथ च अशेषस्य विष्णुरूपा न तु भट्टारकस्य संभारभरणादिबीजभूता आधारशक्तिस्वरूपत्वात्।

पुनः किंभूता। त्रिशूलाकारेत्यादि त्रिशूलाकारं। आदित एकस्वरूपमपि। अग्रतो विभक्ततयावस्थितं च तत्पश्यन्त्यादित्रयं तस्य विमर्शः स एव सखा सहायो येषां ते तेन सखायः सद्दशावाये अनन्तशक्तिमणयस्तेषां प्रभेव प्रभा प्रकाशः तस्याः समुद्भेदः।

कचितत्वं तस्य सामरस्यं समरसत्वं निवातनिस्तरङ्गसमुद्राभ्यन्तस्तरङ्गानुदयवत्परान्तरेव पश्यन्त्यादिसकलशक्तिप्रकाशानामवस्थानमिति यावत्। तदेव प्रचुरं यस्याः सा अनन्तशक्तीनां भासमानत्वेन पश्यन्त्यादित्रयमेव सहायं तत्तद्रूपकचनसमर्थं सर्वशक्तीनां तद्विमर्शाभेदसारत्वात्। अनेन सामरस्येन सर्वशक्तीनां निमेषावसरेऽपि पराशक्तिगर्भ एव निवासो न तु तत्तच्छक्तिविनाशपर्यायप्रलय इति सूचितम्।

ननु सर्वशक्तीनामविनाशवत्त्वे भावस्वीकारस्य सदा सत्त्वापत्त्या अनिर्मोक्षप्रसङ्ग इति चेत्। न। शक्तिशक्तिमतोः सततमेवाभेदस्येह सम्मतत्वात् अशक्तिमत्त्वे शिव इत्यादिनाम्नोऽपि दुर्निवासत्वात्। स्वनिमेषेण शक्तीनामुन्मेषावसरे तत्तन्नामरूपसङ्कलनात्। शक्तिनिमेषेण स्वोन्मेषाभिप्राये तत्तन्नामाद्यनाकलनात्। शक्तिसत्तायामपि शिवाभिन्नत्वेनानिर्मोक्षप्रसङ्गानापत्तेः बन्धमोक्षयोश्चेहाद्वैतदर्शनेषु परमार्थतः सुतरामसत्त्वात्। स्वकल्पितमोहावसर एव द्वैतादिकल्पनया स्वाप्निकपदार्थवत्क्षणमेव स्थितिलब्धेः तदपसरणे च यथाभूतानुभूतपरमार्थदशया बन्धमोक्षादेः सर्वस्यैव स्वकल्पितत्वेन भ्रान्तिसफलत्वात्।

पुनः किंभूता चित्। चैतन्यरूपा स्वविमर्शसारमयी। अत एव एकैव सर्वत्र चित्स्वरूपप्रतिबन्धात्। ननु अजडे चित्स्वरूपत्वमव्यभिचारि जडे तु व्यभिचरत्येवेति चेत्। उच्यते। अजडस्तावच्चित्स्वरूप एवेति प्रतिपन्नमेव जडोऽपि स्वयमचेतमानोऽपि चित्स्वरूपेण चेत्यमानत्वादजड एव। तद्व्यतिरिक्तत्वेन विमर्शानास्पदत्वादप्रकाशत्वापत्त्या सद्रूपतानन्वयादसतोऽसत्तया जड इत्यादिस्वरूपनाम्नोऽपि नितरां दुर्लभत्वात्। अत एवात्रैकैवेत्येवकारोऽन्ययोगव्यवच्छेदकः। अत एव काचन वक्तुमनिर्वचनीया स्वयमनुभवभाव्या यतः

---

2 अर्थार्थे–बीजभूता] marginal insertion G_2 5 विभक्त $G_2Ś_2$] विभक्ति B_4, विभन्तु $Ś_1$ 7 आनुदयवत् $G_2B_4Ś_2$] आनुदयत् $Ś_1$ 8 पश्यन्त्यादि $B_4Ś_2$] पशन्त्यादि G_2, पचन्त्यादि $Ś_1$ 8 तदेव $G_2Ś_1Ś_2$] तदैव B_4 12 भावस्वी–प्रसङ्ग] marginal insertion G_2 15 तत्तन्नामाद्यनाकलनात् $G_2B_4Ś_2$] तत्तन्नामादिनाकलनात् $Ś_1$ 18 भ्रान्ति $Ś_2$] om. G_2 (caused by broken margin, gap indicated by dots in B_4 and $Ś_1$) 20 प्रतिबन्धात् $G_2Ś_1Ś_2$] प्रतिबन्धनात् B_4 21 उच्यते] om. B_4 22 तद्व्यति $B_4G_2Ś_2$] द्व्यति $Ś_1$ 24 वक्तुम् $G_2B_4Ś_2$] न्तुम् $Ś_1$

परमशिवो न निर्वचनीयः द्वैतास्पर्शात्। परशक्तिरपि तद्रूपत्वादनिर्वचनीयैव विज्ञातारमरे केनेत्यादि यत्र हि द्वैतमेवेत्यादि च श्रुतेः।

ननु द्वयोरप्यनिर्वचनीयत्वेन प्राधान्यात्सततं नित्यत्वाच्च परस्परं करणाकरणादीच्छासत्त्वेन विरोध आपतेदिति चेत्। न नाममात्रेण द्वित्वसङ्ख्यावाचकत्वादर्थतश्चैकपदार्थस्वरूपत्वादुन्मेषदशायां शक्तिरूपाकलनान्निमेषदशायां च शिवस्वरूपशेषत्वाद्बहुधैतस्यार्थ-स्य पूर्वं निर्णीतत्वादग्रतोऽपि निर्णीयमानत्वात्। अत एव चानन्ता अनादित्वेनोत्पत्तिसमयानाकलनाद्विनाशस्य सुतरां दूरत एव वर्जितत्वात्।

अथ च अनन्ता निर्निश्चया च। सर्वस्य स्वात्मस्वरूपत्वेन सदाभासमानत्वात्सन्देहादीनां मरीचिकाजलादिवत्सम्मतानामप्यसम्मतत्वात् यतः स्वात्माज्ञानवान्किल हास्यपात्रमेव स्वात्मत्वेन जात्वप्यज्ञानानास्पदत्वात्। ज्ञानी च ज्ञातस्य ज्ञाता हास्यपात्रमेव। अज्ञातं हि जानन्पुरुषार्थमावहति। ज्ञातस्य ज्ञाने को वा पुरुषार्थः। नन्वेवं शास्त्रोपदेशादीनां वैयर्थ्यमिति चेत्। न। स्वकण्ठगतविस्मृतभूषादिन्यायवत्तेषां मोहापसरणमात्रफलत्वात्। यस्यामतं तस्य मतमित्यादिश्रुतेः । यथास्थितस्तथैवास्स्वेत्यादिसूक्तेश्च।

पुनः किंभूता। न उत्तरमधिकं यतः यथाहि तत्त्वान्तराणि परभैरवबोधानुप्रवेशासादिततथाभावसिद्धीनि संविदमधिकयन्ति। न तथा परा परिपूर्णा भैरवसंवित्तस्याः स्वयमनर्गलानपेक्षप्रथाचमत्कारसारत्वात्। १ न उत्तरं प्रश्नप्रतिवचनरूपं यत्र यत एवं महासंवित्सिन्धोरुल्लसदनन्तप्रतिभापर्यन्तधाम्न उल्लस्य प्रश्नप्रतिवचनपात्रं भवति शिष्यः। तदेव वस्तुतस्तत्त्वं सततोदितमिति किमिवाचार्यीयमन्यदनुत्तरं स्यात्। २ उत्तरणमुत्तरः भेदवादाभिमतो मोक्षः स हि वस्तुतो नियतः प्रथमं शरीरप्राणादिभूमिमधिष्ठाय शून्यपदान्तमारोह्य सकलमलक्षयेनाश्रिततत्त्वव्यक्त्याणुरपवृज्यते इति। ३ स ईदृश एव नाभ्यादिस्थानाधिष्ठानक्रमप्राप्त ऊर्ध्वतरणक्रम उत्तरः ४ तथा उत्तरन्त्यत उत्तरो बन्धः। ५ उत्तरणमुत्तरो मोक्षः ६ एवंविधा उत्तरा यत्र न सन्ति उत्तरं च शब्दनं तत्सर्वथेदृशं तादृशमिति व्यवच्छिन्द्यात्

---

1 पर G$_2$B$_4$Ś$_2$] परम Ś$_1$ 3 करणाकरणा B$_4$G$_2$Ś$_2$] करणा Ś$_1$ 4 आपतेदिति B$_4$G$_2$Ś$_2$] आपत्तेरिति Ś$_1$ 5 बहुधैतस्या B$_4$G$_2$Ś$_2$] बहुधैस्तस्य Ś$_1$ 9 ज्ञानवान् B$_4$G$_2$Ś$_2$] ज्ञानान् Ś$_1$ 11 देशादीनां B$_4$G$_2$Ś$_2$] देशानां Ś$_1$ 13 तस्य मतम् G$_2$Ś$_2$] तस्य मतं मतं यस्य न वेद सः Ś$_1$B$_4$ 19 वादाभि G$_2$Ś$_2$] वादिभि B$_4$, वाभि Ś$_1$ 21 उत्तरन्त्यत G$_2$B$_4$Ś$_2$] उतन्त्य Ś$_1$ 22 तत्सर्व B$_4$G$_2$Ś$_2$] ततन्सर्व Ś$_1$

---

2 विज्ञातारमरे केन [विजानीयात्]] *Bṛhadāraṇyakopaniṣad* 4.5.19 2 यत्र हि द्वैतमेव] ibid. 4.5.15 (with *iva* in the vulgate text) 13 यस्यामतं तस्य मतम्] *Kenopaniṣad* 2.3. Ś$_1$ and B$_4$ add the second pāda.

तद्यत्र न भवति ७ अत एव यावदनुत्तरे रूपे मायीयप्रमाता प्रविविक्षेत्तावत्कल्पित एव विशेषात्मनि तत्र त्वकल्पितं यत्समवेतं तद्विना कल्पितरूपा स्फुरणात् तदेव वस्तुतोऽनुत्तरम्। तथा परात्मनः शाक्तशाम्भवादय उत्तराः ते यत्र न उत्तराः जाग्रदादयो वा यत्र न। ८ तथा पश्यन्त्याद्याः शक्तयः उत्तराः ता यत्र न। ९ घोराद्याश्चोत्तराः ता यत्र न। १० परापराद्याश्चोत्तराः ता यत्र न। ११ सर्वशक्तयश्चोत्तरास्ता यत्र न। १२ तथा नोदनं नुत् तया तरणं दीक्षाक्रमेण तरः शिष्यचैतन्ये गुरुश्चैतन्यं प्रेरयति। न तु होमादिविधिना तदेवंविधस्तरस्तरणं यत्र न स्वप्रकाशचैतन्यस्य सर्वव्यापकस्य एवंविधविडम्बनानास्पदत्वात्। १३ तथा अनिति श्वसिति इति क्विपि अन्। अणुरात्मा पुर्यष्टकादिः तथा अननं जीवनं देहाद्यन्तर्गतैवाभिन्नभिन्नशक्त्याद्यहन्ताशून्यप्राया जीवनाख्या वृत्तिर्या शून्यप्रमातेत्यभिहिता तस्यैव उत्तरत्वं सर्वतः परमार्थधियाधिक्यं यत्र शिवैकमयत्वात्। अजडानां तावज्ज्ञानक्रिये एव जीवनं जडानां च जीववदाश्रयत्वं जीवनं। १४ तथा अ इति अमायीयनैसर्गिकमहाप्रकाशविश्रान्तनिस्तरङ्गचित्सिन्धुस्वात्मचमत्काररूपा शान्तोल्लासमयविश्रामर्शनरूपपराहन्ताप्रथमपर्यवसानोभयभूमिगा येयं तस्या एव नुत्। विसर्गान्ता तस्या एव तरः प्लवनं सर्वोपरिवृत्तित्वं यत्र। १५ अविद्यमाना नुत् द्वैतादिप्रेरणा यत्र तदनुत् अतिशयेन अनुत् अनुत्तरं सर्वव्याप्तत्वेनाक्रमिकत्वात्। १६ ईदृशमतिविततार्थमपि शिष्यबोधार्थं संक्षिप्तं षोडशधा निर्णीतमनुत्तरमत एव निरुत्तरं निःशेषेण उत्तरं अनुत्तरत्वादुत्तरान्निर्गतं वा सर्वैरुत्तरं सर्वेभ्य उत्तरं वा सर्वं च तदुत्तरं च वा स्वसमाधारणं विलासेन विलासानां वा भासकत्वं प्रकाशः ततः सकाशात्ततो हेतोर्वा उत्तीर्णा तदुत्क्रम्य तीर्णा तत उच्चैस्तीर्णा च।

पुनः किंभूता। अत एव त्रिकमयैक्यपरसहजौजोविषदा। त्रिकं शिवशक्त्यणुस्वरूपं तत्प्रकृति ऐक्यं यस्य परसहजौजसः तेन विषदा। ननु शिवशक्त्यणुस्वरूपं चेत्त्रिकत्वं तत्रैक्यं कथं त्रिकत्वे ऐक्यासम्भवादिति चेत्। सत्यं किन्तु एतत्त्रिकत्वमेवैक्यं यतोऽत्र शिवशक्त्यणूनां त्रिकत्वं न पृथक्पृथक्पदार्थवाचकं किन्तु पृथक्पृथगवस्थावर्णनार्हत्वेनैकस्यैव परवस्तुनस्तत्तन्नामनिरूपणं शिवः किल पूर्वनिर्णीतपरिपूर्णाहन्ताप्रथासारः। तदभिन्ना च शक्तिः। तयोरनुसन्धाता चाणुः। तदनुसन्धानरहितः स एव जीवत्वादिव्यपदेशभाक्तत्तन्नानाविकल्पपात्रं भवति। तदनुसन्धानेन जलतरङ्गन्यायेन स एव सन्स्वकल्पिताविद्यया

---

1 नुत्तरे] om. G$_2$(damaged margin) 3 ते यत्र न उत्तराः G$_2$Ś$_1$B$_4$] ता यत्र न घोराद्याश्च Ś$_2^{ac}$ om. Ś$_2^{pc}$ 5 उत्तराः G$_2$Ś$_1$Ś$_2$] उत्तरा B$_4$ 7 गुरुश्चैतन्यम् [...] स्तरणं om. Ś$_1$ (gap indicated) 11 क्रिये एव G$_2$Ś$_2$] क्रियैव Ś$_1$B$_4$ 13 गा येयं G$_2$Ś$_2$] गावेयं Ś$_1$B$_4$ 13 विसर्गान्ता Ś$_1$G$_2$Ś$_2$] विसर्गन्ता B$_4$ 18 हेतोर्वा] om. Ś$_1$ 18 तदुत्क्रम्य Ś$_1$B$_4$G$_2$] उत्क्रम्य Ś$_2$ 20 ऐक्यं G$_2$Ś$_1$Ś$_2$] ऐन्यं B$_4$ 22 अवस्थावर्णना Ś$_1$Ś$_2$G$_2$] वर्णना B$_4$ 23 निरूपणं B$_4$G$_2$Ś$_2$] रूपणं Ś$_1$

न स इव नाहमस्मीत्यादि वदन् पुनरपि स्वप्रत्यभिज्ञानेन स एव सः इति न किंचित्परमार्थतस्त्रिकत्वं सर्वस्वरूपस्यैकस्वरूपत्वात्। अत्रिकत्वे चैक्यमपि हास्यावहमेवान्यं विना एकस्य सत एकमिति ज्ञानस्यापि दुर्बोधत्वात् त्रिकमयैक्यं च तत्परं च सहजं च ओजः प्रकाशः स्वशक्तिः स्वबलं वा तेन विषदा मलरहिता विषं मूर्च्छादायित्वेन संसाराख्याविद्या तद्द्याति खण्डयति च।

पुनः कथंभूता सदा उत्तुङ्गः। अन्यव्यतिरिक्तः अभङ्गः अविनाशश्च परहर्षः तस्य स्पन्दः तस्य उदयः तस्मिन्नुद्यता एतेन चिदानन्दाख्ययोरुभयोरपि शक्त्योः समावेशः परायां सङ्कीर्तितः वक्ष्यमाणपश्यन्त्यादित्रये इच्छाज्ञानक्रियाणामनुप्रवेशनिष्पत्तेः।

पुनः किंभूता। तत्तन्माहेश्वरनानाशक्तीनां निमेष एव समुन्मेषः उन्मेष एव च निमेषः तयोस्तत्त्वं तेन तस्मिन्वा उन्मिषिता विकसिता पुनः अतीव सर्वातीता सर्वमतीत्य वर्तमानापि स्वयं सर्वैव समुज्जृम्भमाणा विलसन्ती ये ये भावा उन्मिषितास्तेऽपि तन्मयाः निमिषितास्तदन्तर्भूतत्वात्तन्मया एवेत्यनेन सूचितम्। उन्मेषे निमेषस्तस्मिंश्चोन्मेष इति प्राङ्निर्णीतमेव॥

---

1 इव Ś$_2$B$_4^{pc}$ G$_2$] एव B$_4^{ac}$, initial vowel deleted Ś$_1$ 1 वदन् G$_2$Ś$_2$] वत् Ś$_1$B$_4$ 2 परमार्थतस् B$_4$G$_2$Ś$_2$] परमार्थ Ś$_1$ 2 सर्वस्व–त्वात्] om. Ś$_1$(gap indicated) 2 अत्रिकत्वे चै G$_2$B$_4$Ś$_2$] त्रिकत्वेन्नै Ś$_1$ 4 स्वशक्तिः B$_4$G$_2$Ś$_2$] शक्तिः Ś$_1$ 5 तद्द्याति ख coni.] तद्द्यति ख Ś$_2$, तद्द्या B$_4$, तत्स्या Ś$_1$, om. G$_2$(broken margin, gap indicated Ś$_1$B$_4$) 6 कथंभूता B$_4$G$_2$Ś$_2$] किंभूता Ś$_1$ 7 स्पन्दः तस्य उदयः G$_2$Ś$_2$] तस्य उदयः Ś$_1$, तदुदयः B$_4$ 10 उन्मेष एव च निमेषः] om. Ś$_1$B$_4$ 10 Ś$_2$ next folio continues with स्वविभव 12 तदन्तर् G$_2^{pc}$] ततदन्त B$_4$, तु तदनन्त Ś$_1$

[mūla text, third section]

ओं तत एव स्वस्वविभवानुभवमहेशप्रकाशमाना या बीजप्रथमस्वेदोद्भववत्पश्यन्ती परेच्छाविर्भूता कापीदन्ताविलासान्तर्भाविनी नितरां प्रबलाहन्ताविमर्शनसारान्तरा स्फुरिततत्तद्विशालविशालविशालसप्तप्रमातृघननर्तनमयमध्यमादिशब्दनसङ्केतभूमिरपि तदभूमिः ॥

[commentary]

एवं तावत्परास्वरूपं संगृह्य पश्यन्तीमाविष्करोति तत एवेति तत एव पूर्वप्रकृताया महापरायाः पश्यन्ती अविर्भूतेति सम्बन्धः न तु स्वतः स्वातन्त्र्येण न वानाश्रितात्क्रमापहानेन स्वकरणोल्लङ्घनेन न वा मध्यमादिभ्यो व्युत्क्रमेणेत्याद्यन्ययोगेव्यवच्छिन्नत्वे ऽत्र एवकारः पश्यन्तीमिदन्तामनादृत्य स्वाहन्तामेवा केवलां साक्षात्करोति इति पश्यन्ती आविर्भूतेत्यनेनापि पूर्ववदस्यापि समुत्पत्तिराहित्यमिति सूचितं सदा तदा तदनन्तर्वासत्या एवाकृत्रिमाहन्ता स्वरसचमत्कारसामरस्यभूतत्वमेवास्या आविर्भूतत्वदृष्टिविषयम् [.....] भावभावनलक्षणोपपत्त्वादिविषयम्। कथं बीजप्रथमस्वेदोद्भववत्। बीजाद्यथा प्रथममेव भूम्यन्तरेव बीजस्फोटनं विना बीजाभ्यन्तरेव स्वेदोद्भवः विकसितत्वमिव तद्वत्।

कापीत्यनेनानिर्वाच्या परेच्छा स्वरूपकारणत्वेन पश्यन्ती आविर्भूतेति पूर्वेण सम्बन्धः। कथम्भूता नितरामतिशयेन प्रबला सर्वोत्कृष्टबीजावती याहन्ता परमशिवस्य शिवोऽहमस्मीति सर्वो ममायं विभव इति विमर्शनं विमर्शो नाम विश्वाकारेण विश्वप्रकाशेन विश्वसंहरणेन याहमिति धीर्हृत्स्पन्दस्तस्य सारः सरत्यनेनेति सारः सरणिर्निःसरणमार्गः

1 ओं] om. C_{1-3} 1 महेन $G_2B_3C_{1-3}$] महेश $Ś_1B_4$ 3 सारान्तरा $B_4G_2B_3C_{1-3}$] सारन्तरा $Ś_1$ 3 तत्तद् $Ś_1G_2B_3B_4C_2C_3^{pc}$] तद् C_1, om. C_3^{ac} 3 शब्दन $Ś_1G_2B_3C_{1-3}$] शब्दर B_4 4 तद] तदा (तट?) C_1 5 from here second hand in G_2 6 $Ś_1$ reads पूर्वप्रकृताया महापरायाः पश्यन्तीमाविष्करोति तत एवेति तत एव पूर्वप्रकृताया महापरायाः पश्यन्ती अविर्भूतेति 7 स्वकरणो B_4G_2] स्वकारणो $Ś_1$ 7 अन्ययोगे G_2] अयोगं $Ś_1B_4$ 8 दृत्य $G_2Ś_1$] दृत्यं B_4 9 अस्यापि $Ś_1B_4$] अस्यापि अस्या अपि G_2 9 वासत्या B_4G_2] वापद्या $Ś_1$ 10 (gap marked with five dots in $G_2Ś_1B_4$) 11 कथं बीजाप्रथम] om. $Ś_1$ (gap indicated) 12 भूम्यन्तरेव बीजस्फोटनं विना om. B_4 (gap indicated) 12 कथम्–स्वेदोद्भवः om. $Ś_1$ 12 G_2 ends with तद्वत् 14 शयेन] om. $Ś_1$ (gap indicated)

15 सर्वो ममायं विभव] *Īśvarapratyabhijñākārikā* 4.12

अन्तरमन्तःकरणं यस्याः सदेक्षत बहु स्यां प्रजायेयेति श्रुतेः तथा शिवस्य प्रकाशात्मकस्य विमर्शनं विमर्शशक्तिस्तस्याः प्रसरः प्रथा षड्विंशत्तत्त्वात्मना परिणामः। तथा चोक्तं मृत्युजिद्भट्टारके

ततः प्रवर्तते शक्तिर्लक्ष्यहीना निरामया।
इच्छा सा तु विनिर्दिष्टा ज्ञानरूपा क्रियात्मिका॥

सा योनिः सर्वदेवानां शक्तीनां चाप्यनेकधा।
अग्निषोमात्मिका योनिः तस्यां सर्वं प्रवर्तते॥

इत्युक्तरीत्या एकस्या एव पराशक्तेः इच्छाज्ञानक्रियात्मकत्वेन व्युपदेशसिन्धोः।

अहमेव परो हंसः शिवः परमकारणम्।

इति स्वच्छन्दभट्टारकोक्तनीत्या

तस्य देवादिदेवस्य परबोधस्वरूपिनः।
विमर्शः परमा शक्तिः सर्वज्ञज्ञानशालिनीति

तथेच्छाशक्तिरेव सामरस्यमापन्ना पश्यन्तीरूपेण स्थितेति भावः कथंभूता अकारा क्षकारान्ताश्च ते ते वर्णाः। अकारः परमशिवः अक्षराणामकारोऽस्मि इति श्रीमद्भगवद्वासुदेवोक्तेः क्षकारः पृथ्वीवाचकः तन्त्रान्तरोक्तेः अत एव सर्वे वर्णाः शिवात्मिका इति श्रीसर्ववीरभट्टारकोक्तरित्या च विशन्ति प्रवेशं कुर्वन्ति इति विशाला तथा स्फुरिता तैरेव

---

1 अन्तरमन्तः $Ś_1$] अन्तरन्तः B_4 12 सर्वज्ञज्ञान coni.] सर्वज्ञान $Ś_1B_4$ 15 तन्त्रान्तरोक्तेः coni.] तन्त्रोतरोक्तेः B_4, तन्त्रतरोक्तेः $Ś_1$ 16 रकोक्तरीत्या B_4] रकोक्तेः रीत्या $Ś_1$ 16 विशन्ति B_4] विंशति $Ś_1$ 16 तैरेव $Ś_1$] तैरे B_4

---

1 सदेक्षत बहु स्यां प्रजायेयेति] *Chāndogyopaniṣad* 6.2.3 (with *tad aikṣata* for *sad ekṣata*) 5 ततः …] *Netratantra* 7.36 with *mātra* for *sā tu* 7 तस्यां …] *Netratantra* 7.40 with *tasyāḥ* for *tasyām* 9 अहमेव] *Svacchandatantra* 4.399 11 तस्य देवादि] Quoted by Jayaratha ad *Tantrāloka* 5.77. The *Svacchandatatroddyota* quotes Pādas a–c as from the *Śrīkālikula* with *devāti* in Pāda a and *aviyukto yayā prabhuḥ* as Pāda d. 14 अक्षराणामकारोऽस्मि] *Bhagavadgītā* 10.33 15 सर्वे वर्णाः शिवात्मिका] Quoted in *Tantrālokaviveka* 12.25

वर्णैर्विकचनं ता प्राप्तवती दर्पणमुखन्यायेनाविभक्तं स्वस्वरूपं विश्वोत्तीर्णविश्वमयं पश्यतीति यथार्थनाम्ना प्रोक्षितवती स ऐक्षत बहु स्यामिति श्रुतेः ।

अविभागा तु पश्यन्ती सर्वतः संहृतक्रमः ।
स्वरूपज्योतिरेवान्तः सूक्ष्मा वागनपायिनी ॥

केवलं बुद्ध्युपादाना क्रमरूपानुपातिनी ।
प्राणवृत्तिमतिक्रम्य मध्यमा वाग् प्रवर्तते ॥

स्थानेषु विवृते वायौ कृतवर्णपरिग्रहा ।
वैखरी वाक्प्रयोक्तॄणां प्राणवृत्तिनिबन्धनम् ॥

इति वाक्त्रितयस्य लक्षणादविभागात्तु पश्यन्तीत्यादिना लक्षितां प्रथममेव उन्मिषिता परेच्छात्मिकात्वेन पश्यन्त्याख्या ज्योतिष्ट्वाच्च विशाला विशिष्टदीप्ति विशिष्टदीप्तिमती विचित्ररचनावती च तथा श्रीमालिनीविजयो

परावाक्प्रसरन्तीच्छाज्ञानक्रियारूपतां श्रित्वा क्रमेणाकारादिक्षकारान्तमातृकात्मतापरशिवादिक्षित्यन्तषट्त्रिंशत्तत्त्वात्मस्वरूपेण विशाला विस्तीर्णा विस्तरं प्राप्ता तथा सप्तप्रमातृषु मन्त्रमहेश्वरमन्त्रेश्वरमन्त्रविज्ञानाकलप्रलयाकलसकलशिवभट्टारका इत्येते ये सप्तप्रमातारस्तेषु घनं निरन्तरं यथा तथा नर्तनमयी प्राचुर्ये मयडिति शब्दानुशासनात् नर्तनप्रचुरा पौनःपुन्येन प्रचुरपरिचया बुद्ध्युपादानात् केवलं ज्ञानप्रधाना मध्यमा आदिशब्देन वैखरीत्युपलक्ष्यते विखरे शरीरे विहरतीति वैखरी क्रियाप्रधानां शब्दितः नाम वाक्प्रपञ्चस्तस्य संकेतः प्रकटीकरणं संकेतो नाम नामरूपात्मना घटपटादिनीलपीतादिव्यवहरणात्मकवस्तुजाततदात्मिका वैखरी शब्दानां जननी त्वमत्र भुवने वाग्वादिनीत्युच्यसे त्वत्तः केचन वासवप्रभृतयोऽप्याविर्भवन्ति स्फुटम् । लीयन्ते खलु यत्र कल्पविरमे ब्रह्मादय तेऽप्यमी †त्वं कामिदमित्यरूप† शक्तिः परा गीयसे ।

---

9 त्रितयस्य B_4] तृतयस्य $Ś_1$ 9 भागात्तु B_4] भागत्त $Ś_1$ 10 विशिष्टदीप्ति B_4] विशिष्टदीपि $Ś_1$ 11 विजयो] (one line with dots indicating a gap) B_4 12 कारादि $Ś_1$] कादि B_4 17 शब्दितः B_4] शब्दत $Ś_1$ 20 स्फुटम्] End of $Ś_1$ इति शमिति कल्पवृक्षव्याख्या श्रीमत्साहिबकौलविरचिता 20 ब्रह्मादय coni.] ब्रह्माद B_4 21 गीयसे] B_4 ends with *iti śāstram*

---

2 स ऐक्षत बहु स्याम्] *Chāndogyopaniṣad* 6.2.3 (with *tad aikṣata* for *sad ekṣata*) 3 अविभागा तु पश्यन्ती [...] प्राणवृत्तिनिबन्धनम्] *Vākyapadīya* 1.167, 166, 165

Bibliography

Manuscripts of the *Kalpavṛkṣa*

B_3	Staatsbibliothek zu Berlin, Preußischer Kulturbesitz, Hs. or. 12460	Śāradā, paper
B_4	Staatsbibliothek zu Berlin, Preußischer Kulturbesitz, Hs. or. 12666	Nāgarī and Śāradā, paper
G_2	Niedersächsische Staats- und Universitätsbibliothek, Göttingen, Cod. Ms. Sansc. Vish 203	Śāradā, paper
Ś$_1$	Dogra Art Museum, Jammu, 425	Śāradā, birch bark
Ś$_2$	Oriental Research Library, Srinagar, Acc. 1353	Śāradā, paper

The Cloths

C_1	Oriental Research Library, Srinagar, Acc. 8747	Śāradā, cloth
C_2	Oriental Research Library, Srinagar, Acc. 2190	Śāradā, cloth
C_3	Oriental Research Library, Srinagar, Acc. 2189	Nāgarī, cloth

Printed Sanskrit Editions

Anuttarāṣṭika Ed. K. C. PANDEY: *Abhinavagupta.* Varanasi: Chaukhamba Amarabharati Prakashan 1963, p. 943f.

Īśvarapratyabhijñākārikā 1.1 → RAFFAELE TORELLA: *The Īśvarapratyabhijñākārikā of Utpaladeva with the Author's Vṛtti. Critical edition and annotated translation.* Rome: IsMEO 1994.

Ṛgveda THEODOR AUFRECHT: *Die Hymnen des Ṛigveda.* Bonn: Marcus 1877.

Kaṭhopaniṣad → OLIVELLE: *The early Upaniṣads*

Kāvyamīmāṃsā *Kāvyamīmāṃsā of Rājaśékhara.* Ed. C. D. DALAL and K. S. RAMASWAMI SASTRI SIROMANI Baroda: Oriental Institute 1934.

Kāvyānuśāsana *The Kāvyānuśāsana of Hemachandra with his own gloss.* Bombay: Nirnaya Sagar Press. Reprint New Delhi 1986.

Kirātārjunīya Ed. PAṆḌIT DURGĀPRASĀD and KĀŚINĀTH PĀṆḌURANG PARAB. Bombay: Nirṇaya Sāgara 1889.

Kumārasambhava *Vallabhadeva's Kommentar (Śāradā-Version) zum Kumārasambhava des Kālidāsa.* Ed. M. S. NARAYANA MURTI. Wiesbaden: Steiner 1980.

Citsphārasārādvaya → HANNEDER: *Sāhib Kaula's Works.*

Chāndogyopaniṣad → OLIVELLE: *The early Upaniṣads*

Tantrāloka *Tantrāloka of Abhinavagupta with the commentary (-viveka) of Rājānaka Jayaratha.* Ed. MUKUND RĀM ŚĀSTRĪ. Bombay: Nirnaya Sagar Press and Srinagar, 1918–38.

Taittirīyopaniṣad → OLIVELLE: *The early Upaniṣads*

Dakṣiṇamūrtistotra *The Dakshinamurti-Stotra of Sri Sankaracarya.* Ed. A. MAHADEVA SASTRI. Mysore: Government Branch Press 1895.

Devīnāmavilāsa *The Devīnāmavilāsa. By Sāhib Kaul.* Ed. by MADHUSŪDAN KAUL SHĀSTRĪ. Lahore: Manohar 1942. (Kashmir Series of Texts and Studies LXIII).

Devīmāhātmya Lakhnau 1955 (traditional poṭhi).

Nijātmabodha → HANNEDER: *Sāhib Kaula's Works.*

Netratantra *Netratantra with the commentary (Netroddyota) of Rājānaka Kṣemarāja.* Ed. Madhusūdan Kaul Śāstrī. Bombay: Nirnaya Sagar Press and Srinagar, 1926 and 1939.

Nyāyasūtra Walter Ruben: *Die Nyāyasūtra's: Text, Übers., Erl. u. Glossar.* Leipzig: Deutsche Morgenländische Gesellschaft / F. A. Brockhaus 1928.

Bṛhadāraṇyakopaniṣad → Olivelle: *The early Upaniṣads*

Bhāgavatapurāṇa Ed. Narayaṇa Rāma Ācārya. Bombay: Satyabhama Bhai Pandurang 1950.

Mahābhārata Ed. V. S. Sukthankar et al.. Pune: BORI 1927–1959.

Mokṣopāya *Mokṣopāya. Das Fünfte Buch. Upaśāntiprakaraṇa. Kritische Edition. Von Susanne Krause-Stinner und Peter Stephan.* Wiesbaden: Harrassowitz 2013.

Raghuvaṃśa *The Raghupañcika of Vallabhadeva: being the earliest commentary on the Raghuvamsá of Kalidasa.* Ed. Dominic Goodall and Harunaga Isaacson. Groningen: Forsten 2003.

***Rājataraṅgiṇī* (Śrīvara)** *Rājataraṅgiṇī of Śrīvara and Śuka.* Ed. by Srikanth Kaul. Hoshiarpur: Vishveshvaranand Institute 1966.

Vākyapadīya *Bhartṛharis Vākyapadīya.* Ed. Wilhelm Rau. Wiesbaden: Steiner 1977.

Śārikāstava → Hanneder: *Sāhib Kaula's Works.*

Śivajīvadaśaka → Hanneder: *Sāhib Kaula's Works.*

Śivamahimnaḥstotra W. Norman Brown: *The Mahimnastava or Praise of Shiva's Greatness.* Poona: American Institute of Indian Studies 1965.

Śivaśaktivilāsa → Hanneder: *Sāhib Kaula's Works.*

Śivasūtra *Śivasūtravārttika of Bhāskara.* Ed. Jagadish Chandra Chatterji. Srinagar 1916.

Śivastotrāvalī *Śivastotrāvalī, a compilation of the devotional verse of Utpaladeva, with the commentary (-vivṛti) of Kṣemarāja.* Ed. Rājānaka Lakṣmaṇa. Varanasi: Chowkhamba Sanskrit Series Office, 1964.

Śrīkaṇṭhacarita *Śrīmaṅkhakakaviviracitaṃ śrīkaṇṭhacaritam. Jonarājakṛtayā ṭīkayā sametam.* Ed. PAṆḌIT DURGĀPRASĀD and KĀŚĪNĀTH PAṆḌURANG PARAB. Bombay: Nirnaya Sagar 1887. Reprint. Delhi 1983.

Śvetāśvataropaniṣad → OLIVELLE: *The early Upaniṣads*

Saccidānandakandalī → HANNEDER: *Sāhib Kaula's Works.*

Sarasvatīkaṇṭhābharaṇa *The Saraswatī Kaṇṭhābharaṇa by Dhāreshvara Bhojadeva with the Commentary of Rāmsinha (I–III) and Jagaddhara (IV).* (Kāvyamālā 94). Bombay: Nirnaya Sagar 1934.

— *Sarasvatīkaṇṭhābharaṇe śrīmadbhojanarendraviracite paricchedatrayaṃ. paṇḍitavaryaratneśvaramiśraviracitayā ratnadarpaṇākhyayā vyākhyayānugataṃ.* Ed. DRĀVIḌAVIREŚVARA ŚĀSTRĪ. Kāśī: Jainaprabhākara vaiśākha sudi 8 bhaume saṃvatsare 1843 [=1921 A.D.].

Sahajārcanāṣaṣṭikā → HANNEDER: *Sāhib Kaula's Works.*

Saundaryalaharī *Saundaryalaharī.* Ed. A. KUPPUSWAMI. Delhi: Nag 1991.

Spandakārikā *Spandakārikā with the commentary (-vivṛti) of Rāmakaṇṭha.* Ed. J. C. CHATTERJI. Srinagar: Research Department Jammu and Kashmir 1913.

Hastāmalaka Ed. E. B. COWELL: The *Hastāmalaka.* In: *Indian Antiquary* 9 (1880), pp. 25–27.

Secondary Literature

Battistini, Alessandro. "Citrakāvya in Manuscripts: the case of Ānandavardhana's Devīśataka." In: *Kriti Rakshana* 9.5 (2014), pp. 7–11.

Böhtlingk, Otto. *Bṛhadāraṇjakopanishad in der Mādhyaṃdina-Rezension.* St. Petersburg, 1889.

Dencker, Klaus Peter. *Optische Poesie. Von den prähistorischen Schriftzeichen bis zu den digitalen Experimenten der Gegenwart.* Pictura et poesis 1. Berlin: de Gruyter, 2011.

Ehlers, Gerhard. *Indische Handschriften. Teil 19: Die Śāradā-Handschriften der Sammlung Janert der Staatsbibliothek zu Berlin – Preußischer Kulturbesitz.* Verzeichnis der Orientalischen Handschriften in Deutschland 2.19. Stuttgart: Steiner, 2016.

Ernst, Ulrich. *Carmen figuratum: Geschichte des Figurengedichts von den antiken Ursprüngen bis zum Ausgang des Mittelalters.* Pictura et poesis 1. Köln [u.a.]: Böhlau, 1991.

— ed. *Visuelle Poesie: historische Dokumentation theoretischer Zeugnisse. Band 1: Von der Antike bis zum Barock.* Berlin [u.a.]: de Gruyter, 2012.

Formigatti, Camillo A. "Guṭakas between Book Cultures. The Voelter Manuscripts in the Tübingen Library." In: *Die 1000 Namen Vishnus. Sanskrit-Handschriften aus der Sammlung Heide und Wolfgang Voelter.* Ed. by Frank Köhler and Heike Oberlin. Tübingen: Museum der Universität Tübingen, 2020, pp. 64–90.

Gerow, Edwin. *A glossary of Indian figures of speech.* Vol. 16. Walter de Gruyter, 2012.

Hahn, Michael. "Der Bhāṣāśleṣa. Ein Besonderheit kaschmirischer Dichter und Poetiker?" In: *Highland philology: results of a text-related Kashmir Panel at the 31st DOT, Marburg 2010.* Ed. by Roland Steiner. Studia Indologica Universitatis Halensis 4. Halle: Universitätsverl. Halle-Wittenberg, 2012, pp. 77–105.

Hanneder, Jürgen. *Abhinavagupta's Philosophy of Revelation. An Edition and Annotated Translation of Mālinīślokavārttika I, 1–399.* Groningen, 1998.

— *Studies on the Mokṣopāya.* Wiesbaden: Otto Harrassowitz Verlag, 2006.

— "Pre-modern Sanskrit Authors, Editors and Readers." In: *Indic Manuscript Cultures through the Ages: Material, Textual, and Historical Investigations.* Vol. 14. Walter de Gruyter GmbH & Co KG, 2017, p. 223.

Hanneder, Jürgen. *To edit or not to edit*. Pune Indological Series 1. New Delhi: Aditya Prakashan, 2017.
— "Śārikā's Mantra." In: *Śaivism and the Tantric Traditions: Essays in Honour of Alexis Sanderson*. Leiden, 2020, pp. 347–361.
— *Sahib Kaula's Works*. Forthcoming.
Hodgson, Phyllis. *The Cloud of Unknowing and the Book of Privy Counselling*. Oxford: Early English Text Society, 1944.
Jha, Kalanath. *Figurative poetry in Sanskrit literature*. Motilal Banarsidass Publ., 1975.
— "Sanskrit Citrakāvyas and the Western Pattern Poem: A Critical Appraisal." In: *Visible Language* 20.1 (1986), 109ff.
— "Sanskrit Citrakāvyas and the Western Pattern Poem." In: *Pattern Poetry. Guide to an Unknown Literature*. New York, 1987, pp. 221–229.
Jordan Gschwend, Annemarie and Johannes Beltz, eds. *Elfenbeine aus Ceylon: Luxusgüter für Katharina von Habsburg (1507 - 1578)*. Zürich: Museum Rietberg, 2010.
Lienhard, Siegfried. "Text-Bild-Modelle der klassischen indischen Dichtung." In: *Siegfried Lienhard: Kleine Schriften*. Wiesbaden, 2007, pp. 133–158.
Olivelle, Patrick. *The Early Upaniṣads*. New York, 1998.
Pāṇḍeya, Janārdana, ed. *Śaivādvayaviṃśatikā*. 1. saṃskaraṇa. Vidyāpīṭha-granthamālā ; 1. Navadehalī: Śrīlālabahāduraśāstrirāṣṭriyasaṃskṛtavidyāpīṭha, 1997.
Ratié, Isabelle. "Pāramārthika or apāramārthika? On the ontological status of separation according to Abhinavagupta." In: *Puṣpikā. Volume 1*. Oxford, 2009, pp. 381–405.
Ratnakaṇṭha, Rājānaka. *Ratnakaṇṭhas Stotras: Sūryastutirahasya, Ratnaśataka und Śambhukṛpāmanoharastava*. Ed. by Jürgen Hanneder, Stanislav Jager, and Alexis Sanderson. Indologica Marpurgensia 5. München: Kirchheim, 2013.
Rühl, Meike. "Panegyrik im Quadrat: Optatian und die intermedialen Tendenzen des spätantiken Herrscherbildes." In: *Millennium* 3.1 (2006), pp. 75–101.
Sanderson, Alexis. "The Śaiva Religion among the Khmers." In: *Bulletin de l'Ecole française d'Extrême-Orient* 90 (2003), pp. 349–462.
— "Kashmir." In: *Brill's Encyclopedia of Hinduism*. Vol. 1. Leiden: Brill, 2009, pp. 99–126.
Slaje, Walter. *Upanischaden. Arkanum des Veda*. Frankfurt am Main, 2009.

Stainton, Hamsa. *Govinda Kaula: Evidence for His Dating, Lineage, and Literary Activity*. Forthcoming.

Vose, Steven M. “Jain Uses of Citrakāvya and Multiple-Language Hymns in Late Medieval India: Situating the Laghukāvya Hymns of Jinaprabhasūri in the ‘Assembly of Poets’.” In: *International Journal of Hindu Studies* 20.3 (2016), pp. 309–337.

Williams, Tyler Walker. “Sacred sounds and sacred books: A history of writing in Hindi.” PhD thesis. Columbia University, 2014.

Index

Advaita Vedānta, 1, 28
ākāracitra, 48
Arabic, 42

bandha, 47
bhāṣāśleṣa, 4
Bilhaṇa, 62
birch bark, 7, 11
brahmādvaya, 91

carmen cancellatum, 55
carmen figuratum, 54
citrakāvya, 4, 45, 46
Citsphārasārādvaya, 1

Devīnāmavilāsa, 1
Dīlārāma Kaula, 44
dvaita, 93

eGangotri, 1

Gaṇeśa Kaula, 24, 25
Gittergedicht, 54
gomūtrika, 50, 52

Hrabanus Maurus, 56
Hṛllekhāpaddhati, 1

intexts, 54

Jaswant Singh
=Yaśovatsiṃha, 15

Kabir, 42
Kalpavṛkṣa
aerial roots, 15, 53
tree image, 15, 23, 38, 57
Kṛṣṇadāsa, 42

mahādvaya, 91
mantroddhāra, 2
maruvāṭa, 15
Marvar, 15
Mithila, 44
Mokṣopāya, 17
Muktabodha Digital Library, 11
Mukunda Kaula, 25

Nijātmabodha, 2

parākhyā, 90
Persian, 42
Pratyabhijñā, 28

Ranbir Singh, 25, 26

Ratnakaṇṭha, 55

śabdabrahman, 57
Saccidānandakandalī, 1, 16
Sahajārcanāṣaṣṭikā, 2
Sāhib Kaula
    garden, 13
    name, 1
Śārikāstava, 2
Śivadṛṣṭi, 18
śivādvaya, 91
Śivajīvadaśaka, 2
Śivaśaktivilāsa, 2
Spandakārikā, 18, 21
Śrīvidyānityapūjāpaddhati, 1
Sūrdās, 42
susvatantra, 89
svasvatantra, 89
svātantrya, 91
Śyāmāpaddhati, 1, 25

turaṅga, 50

Utpaladeva, 28

Vidyādhara Kaula, 25
virodhābhāsa, 19
vivarta, 91

Yaśovat Siṃha, 61
Yaśovatsiṃha, 13, 15
Yogavāsiṣṭha, 17, 90

INDICA ET TIBETICA

MONOGRAPHIEN ZU DEN SPRACHEN UND LITERATUREN
DES INDO-TIBETISCHEN KULTURRAUMES

Begründet von
Michael Hahn

Herausgegeben von
Jürgen Hanneder, Jens-Uwe Hartmann,
Konrad Klaus und Roland Steiner

Band 60

Indica et Tibetica Verlag
Marburg 2021

Sāhib Kaula's Tree of Languages